Billy Graham
Evangelistic Association

April 2005

Dear Friend,

It is my privilege to present to you this special commemorative edition of *God in the Garden* by Curtis Mitchell.

This eyewitness account of our 1957 New York Crusade is a wonderful reminder of how God worked in response to the faithful prayers of His people. This volume commemorates not an event or work by individuals, but a profound move of God that changed many lives and affected an entire region.

I believe you will be blessed as you read stories of people who made decisions for Christ during the crusade. You will see how prayer was a vital foundation and how God's people united in their efforts to impact the city for Christ.

I urge you to lift up New York City in prayer even as you praise God for His faithfulness demonstrated in the pages of this book.

It is always an honor to serve you and help you in your Christian walk, and we appreciate knowing how our ministry has touched your life. If you need prayer or other assistance, call us anytime at 1-877-247-2426.

Sincerely,

Billy Graham

2005 COMMEMORATIVE EDITION

GOD
IN THE
GARDEN

THE STORY OF BILLY GRAHAM'S
FIRST NEW YORK CRUSADE

BY CURTIS MITCHELL

This special commemorative edition is published by the
Billy Graham Evangelistic Association with permission
from Doubleday & Company, Inc.

Decision magazine, published 11 times a year by the Billy Graham Evangelistic Association (BGEA), includes inspiring evangelistic and spiritual growth articles and updates about the current work of BGEA. Testimonies from BGEA ministries both educate and spark ideas for local evangelism through the local church. To receive a free issue of *Decision* magazine, call toll-free 1-877-247-2426, or write to Billy Graham Evangelistic Association, 1 Billy Graham Parkway, Charlotte, NC 28201-0001. Ask for special offer BX05X0GIG.

A Message from Billy Graham

The New York Crusade is history. We may not know the full extent of its influence on the lives of people living in metropolitan New York for many years. We do know that thousands of individuals made commitments for Christ.

One of those who watched the unfolding drama of God's workings in our largest city was Curtis Mitchell, feature writer for the *American Weekly* magazine. He has been a frequent visitor to our crusades for a number of years and, having been reared in the home of a minister, has more than a passing interest in evangelism.

During the New York Crusade, he sat in the press section night after night. He interviewed countless persons whose lives were touched by the crusade. As an eyewitness, a keen observer, and analyst of Christian events, he is well qualified to write this documentary story.

He tells of the lives of people that were changed. He reports on the behind-the-scenes contributions of team members, committees, and thousands of volunteers. In print, he recreates significant moments in our Garden services, at the Yankee Stadium, and Times Square.

I am sure that Mr. Mitchell joins me in the hope that those who read this volume might come to a clearer understanding of the objectives of our New York Crusade, and that they will comprehend better the nature of the impact of God's message on our audiences. Most of all, however, it is our hope that GOD IN THE GARDEN will have a special meaning for every reader, whether or not he attended our crusade in person or via television, to the end that the blessings experienced by so many in New York might have a reality in other hearts and lives.

BILLY GRAHAM
1957

GOD IN THE GARDEN

1

This is a story about the people who, with God's help, created a midsummer miracle in Manhattan where 56,000 made decisions for Christ...

On the evening of September 1, 1957, Dr. Billy Graham faced the final and largest audience of his New York Crusade at an outdoor rally in Times Square. An estimated 125,000 people jammed Broadway from curb to curb and overflowed into a dozen side streets.

It was his one hundredth service. For 110 days, through 97 meetings in Madison Square Garden, he had battled the devil in the metropolis known as "the graveyard of evangelists." His only weapons were prayer and repeated declarations of God's love and eventual judgment.

He had fought a good fight. It had sliced eighteen pounds off his lean, weary frame. By midnight he was aboard the Piedmont Limited, hurrying home to his family in North Carolina.

He left an amazing legacy to the city that has been called Sodom-on-the-Subway.

His New York Crusade broke all records for organized evangelistic crusades.

It ran longer.

It attracted more people.

It resulted in more converts.

It cost more money, almost $2,500,000.

Extraordinary figures document the story:

Two million people heard him face to face at either Madison Square Garden meetings or other rallies.

More than 56,000 men, women, and young people came forward and made decisions for Christ.

Of these, 22,000 were under twenty-one.

Over 2,000 were college students from the New York area.

9

More than 500 were from the theater and allied professions.

The average attendance, night after night, through the hottest months of the summer, was 17,828.

A single service at the Yankee Stadium was attended by 100,-000 people, the largest crowd in the history of that citadel of baseball, and over 20,000 others had to be turned away.

An estimated 96,000,000 people viewed one or more of the fourteen Saturday-night coast-to-coast telecasts from the Garden.

A harvest of at least 65,000 souls was gleaned from those telecasts, as was attested by letters from people who certified their decision to accept and follow Christ.

But Billy Graham's greatest success lay in other directions.

The International News Service sent its ace reporter, Phyllis Battelle, into Manhattan at the end of the crusade for the purpose of evaluating Graham's achievement. She reported:

"The powerful evangelist bequeaths two gifts to this polyglot town:

"A dedicated fellowship of more than 50,000 'spiritual babies' newly converted to Christ, commissioned to spread love and battle sin.

"And an all-new concept and privilege to the people of New York to discuss religion without smirking, attend church without apology, and read the Bible without feeling vaguely like a fanatic."

She told of the raised eyebrows and jeers that greeted Graham on his arrival, and the subsequent change of climate.

"Suddenly it seemed like every man's sister was attending crusade meetings regularly, and making a 'decision for Christ,' and appearing almost divinely happy. . . . Sect by sect, class by class, creed by creed, people began to join Graham—or at least to talk about him—and the effect spread around the city until finally it seemed to touch the lives of millions."

Amazingly, boys and girls on dates carried Bibles with them.

Teen-agers were seen on Manhattan subways reading pocket Testaments.

A bus driver on a cross-town route opened a Bible and read in it at every red light or traffic jam. "I went forward the second night," he announced proudly to anyone interested.

A visitor who left his car in a crowded parking lot across from the Garden tried to make a joke with the colored attendant. "Billy Graham must be making a fortune for you," he said.

The attendant replied, "Billy Graham will make a fortune for anyone who will listen to him preach."

Busses rolled along throughways, wearing signs that said, "On our way to hear Billy Graham." After the service, with the sign reversed to read, "We have heard Billy Graham," the night was filled with Gospel music.

A famous psychiatrist came to the Garden four nights straight, taking notes. On the fourth night he went forward at Graham's invitation to make a decision for Christ. "I came to analyze," he said, "but I learned that I was the one being analyzed."

Did he touch people, really? Did Billy Graham, sincere and devout as he undoubtedly was, pour his message into enough souls to make a difference?

People began asking that question with the first meeting on May 15. Psychology professors from New York universities sent their students into Garden crowds with questionnaires designed to produce a scientific answer. Editors dispatched their reporters to the homes of converts. Pastors, counseling new members, probed their hearts and dedication. Churchgoers, seeing new faces in once empty pews, wondered.

Is there an answer?

Not finally, not today! Billy Graham told his audience on his last night at the Garden:

"We are praying that forces will be starting here that in the next five years will make an impact on this community.

"I believe there is a spirit of revival today in America.

"I believe that history will say that 1957 was the year of spiritual awakening.

"Also, history proves that there is a time lag between spiritual awakenings and their impact on society. When John Wesley died, nobody in that time would have said it was a period of revival. It took twenty-five to fifty years for the eighteenth-century revival to make its impact on British society.

"And yet history says today that it was probably the greatest and most effective revival of all time. If you'd gone to Britain when Wesley and Whitfield were preaching, you'd have seen a person in prayer here and another one there and you would have

11

said, 'Why, nothing is going on. Just two or three people gathered in prayer. Nothing going on!'

"And yet, certain forces had started.

"I believe that God today is shaping a new generation of men and women who believe in God.

"I believe that the impact will be felt in days to come!"

At that same final Garden service, thin but amazingly fit and dynamic, he revealed the core of his hope for revival in our time. He knew that the titantic city in which he had preached looked the same on the surface. Apparently his labors had only riffled its sinful currents. But he recalled another age with these dramatic words:

"New York probably looks the same. The crowds still throng Times Square. There are still people going to night clubs. There's still lots of crime in the city.

"Yes, but there is one difference. One tremendous difference! That difference is in the lives of thousands of men and women who will never be the same.

"When Jesus died on the cross, the ruined colony of Palestine went on just the same. Everybody said, 'Why, nothing has happened. Just a man executed.' But he left behind some dedicated men who were used of God to change the world."

Where are the dedicated men and women left by the New York Crusade? Who are they? It is a fair question. It was asked by many newsmen and editors through May, June, July, and August of 1957.

And here are some of the answers:

A recent college graduate, one who had tried to commit suicide, bared her soul in these touching words:

"On July 17, I made my decision.

"I had gone to church, taught Sunday school, and been president of the Young People's Group. But I never really knew Christ. I went away to college . . . I was an agnostic. Every day saw me getting deeper in sin and accepting dark philosophies. I became so confused—with nowhere to turn—I had a nervous breakdown and tried suicide.

"I was brought home from school to see a psychiatrist. After two months I returned to college and was able to finish school. That was six months ago, but the visits to the doctor continued. Inside, there remained a constant turmoil, bewilderment, and gnawing of conscience.

"Then Dr. Graham came to New York. I went to hear him eight times before making my decision. It is astounding how much my life has altered already. I have never known such peace and happiness. I now find joy in living.

"My parents and I have realized that now I no longer need a psychiatrist, so yesterday Mother prayed and asked God what was the right thing to do. Then she heard a voice, which she knew to be God's, saying that since I accepted Christ, I no longer needed the doctor's help, that God had healed my mind and soul and would continue to protect me. Already God has helped me so much. . . ."

A young pharmacist, married and with two children of five and seven, was drifting rapidly toward financial and moral bankruptcy. He was a poor father, husband, and businessman. His neighborhood friends watched his decline helplessly. When his wife said that she was about ready to seek a divorce, they agreed that it was justified. One Saturday he tuned his TV set to the crusade broadcast. He was a Como fan, but the picture of nineteen thousand people listening to so earnest an advocate fascinated him. He sat quietly through the meeting and then went to bed without saying a word to his puzzled wife.

Next day he disappeared. Nobody knew where he had gone, neither his family nor his employees at the drugstore he owned. He was in New York, attending the crusade. That night he went forward and accepted Christ as his Savior.

Returning home, he said, "I am a Christian. I have given my life to Christ."

"I don't believe it," his wife said.

They talked all that day and the next. Again he visited New York and returned home refreshed and invigorated.

"We all need Christ," he told his wife. "If we all accept Him, you and the two children, we can make a go of things. I'm different. I know I'm different. Will you go to New York with me and let me prove it?"

His third trip, that entire family walked down the long Garden aisle to stand before Billy Graham and dedicated itself to God's service. In this man's home today there is Bible reading and prayer at every meal. He has sold his drugstore and is planning to enter a seminary to prepare for the ministry, for that is what he feels God wants him to do.

A New York policeman answered a routine call one night in July. A husband and wife were fighting noisily in their apartment. Neighbors wanted the police to break it up. When he arrived he faced the usual squalid result of cramped quarters, inadequate income, and frayed nerves. The wife had gone out dancing with a friend. The husband had gone after her, brought her home, torn off her clothes, and then torn up every dress in her closet.

The officer knew that an arrest would not help matters. He also knew that Billy Graham had just preached a powerful sermon on the home. "I'll let you off," he told the couple, "if you will agree to go to the Garden and hear Billy Graham. How about it?"

"What's the use?" the man demanded. "She's proved she's no good."

The officer read to them from his pocket Testament. He quoted chapter and verse, as he had heard Billy do. He concluded, "I've got a night off this week. Let's all go hear Billy Graham at the Garden."

That night, when the evangelist gave the invitation, that husband and wife were among the first to go forward, and to register for the Bible course for new Christians that would teach them how to live for God in peace with each other and their community.

During those invitations the very young went forward smilingly, and teen-agers in shyness, and the young married ones holding hands, and the aged most often with tears on their cheeks.

One night one of the aged was a giant of a man, tall and lean like a pioneer, with a face that was a map of life's perplexities. He went to the counseling room in the basement of the Garden, along with hundreds of others, where a counselor came to his side to ask questions designed to prove the inquirer's responsibility for his decision.

The old man said, "My boy, I have been a missionary for twenty-five years."

The young counselor, a seminary student, said, "Sir, I feel that you should be counseling me. What can I say to a man of your experience? But will you tell me, please, why did you come forward tonight?"

14

The old missionary's eyes were troubled. "My mission work was fruitful once. But I felt the power of God leave my ministry a few years ago. I didn't know why. Tonight, listening to Billy, I know at least why I'm accomplishing so little. I have been seeking the praise of men instead of the blessing of God."

"But was it necessary to come forward publicly, sir?"

The old man said, "When Billy gave the invitation, I felt an urge to confess my sin. I hesitated. What would people think? Many in this audience know me and know of my twenty-five years in the mission field. Then I realized that I had worried too long about what people might think. My duty was clear. I had to seek God's forgiveness. I left my seat. It was hard, but it was the only thing to do."

On a memorable evening the wife of one of America's richest men, a family famous in business, sports, and the arts, left her seat and quietly joined the throng of those who stood before Graham's pulpit. Though impeccably dressed, she would have escaped notice if a member of the Graham team had not recognized her.

He hurried to Ruth Graham, who was in the audience, and suggested that the distinguished inquirer might need special help. And so it was that a minister's mate was able to help a millionaire's wife to put her trust in Jesus Christ to solve her grievous problems.

The mother of a notoriously unstable movie beauty went forward at the invitation on another night. Later she returned, bringing her celebrated daughter. This girl had been pictured in every tabloid and headlined in every fan magazine. She had played exotic roles in million-dollar movies and romanced with multimillionaire playboys. But her life had become one disaster after another. Broken and beaten, she had sought refuge in various sanitariums.

At the Garden she listened attentively, almost like a child. Graham's simple message, his promise of God's love and forgiveness, his appeal to her will instead of her emotions, was something new and hopeful. That night she found the ultimate therapy and accepted Christ as her Savior.

"I wish we could have heard Dr. Graham ten years ago," her mother said. "If we had, our troubles would have never begun. But even now, we have found the strength to face our future."

But not all the drama of being born again was played against the backdrop of the Garden. With the first Saturday television broadcast, the impact of the New York Crusade fell upon millions of homes.

A minister in High Point, North Carolina, wrote to Graham about an old man who attended church but had never made a profession of faith. They had talked and argued the need of a decision many times, but the aged man would make no decision. One Saturday night he listened to the crusade hour on television. As the program went off the air, he began to sob.

His wife asked, "What's wrong, dear? Why do you cry?"

He said, "I have given my heart to Christ. I have finally given my heart to Christ."

Next morning when she awoke, he was not in his bed. She found him in the garden among his flowers. He was lying with his face against the mother earth, dead of a heart attack.

The minister wrote, "It is wonderful to know that he was called into the presence of God after having made his decision rather than before. The story ends on a high note of victory, for now the wife and all three children are attending church regularly. Thank you again for what you are doing for the Lord today when the needs of the world are so great."

Television was a new tool in the Graham method for spreading God's word. Nobody really knew what it could do. Nobody was prepared for what did happen.

A skeptical newsman said, "You're wasting your money. Who's going to listen to a preacher on Saturday when he can hear Como or Gleason? And what if a few lonely souls do tune in? What can they do about it?"

Weeks later, that newsman found out. Letters addressed to Billy Graham came from all over America describing unprecedented spiritual adventures. A member of the Graham team handed them over, saying:

"These are some of the lonely souls you talked about. Ten thousand a day are writing us. Read what they say! I dare you!"

From Baltimore, Maryland . . . "For over two years now since my little girl was paralyzed in her left leg, I have been trying to lead a better life and all my prayers were mostly please God heal my little girl. But tonight after listening to you I know her soul is more important. Please pray for me to be able to help bring my children *and* my husband and myself to the feet of Jesus."

From Detroit, Michigan . . . "Your program has brought me into the fold—as an atheist, agnostic pagan. Your examples and comparisons are so easy to understand. Tomorrow for the first time in about eight to ten years I shall go to church."

From El Monte, California . . . "Two weeks ago tonight as I listened to you I knelt down and asked forgiveness for my sins and accepted Christ into my life. Two months ago my husband died very suddenly of a heart attack. We had lived for each other for over thirty-one years and the shock was so great that I lost all interest in life and all incentive to carry on. Since accepting Christ I am beginning to see a purpose and have hope in my heart again. Thank you so very much."

Jersey City, New Jersey . . . "My husband left me and my two small boys about six months ago. He is in love with another woman and wants a divorce. We are in our middle twenties and had been happy for five years. At first I was very despondent and felt I had nothing left to live for even though I love my children. I had never prayed much but I started to then and I found unbelievable peace of mind. Then I heard you on television. You helped me realize that my problem was really small, that the salvation of my soul was much more important. God through you has given me the faith to face the future. With Christ guiding me, I have no fear but that I'll find the right way."

Jamaica, New York . . . "When I first heard about your crusade, I was skeptical of its results. I thought you were selling religion like tooth paste. I was hopelessly hardened against all truth. My intellect mocked the simple and seemingly foolish. Tonight I stumbled on to your program and decided to listen to you 'play upon the emotions of the ignorant.' As time went on I no longer was aware of you. I heard God talking to me and He said, 'Forget, forget all your Doctrine and let your heart come to Me and be cleansed.' I cried and am still crying tears of joy, because I feel alive. It was simple—just accept Christ into your heart."

Vallejo, California . . . "I have been watching for the last four weeks. You brought me to the Lord three weeks ago. My whole outlook on life has changed. Thank the Lord. With Him by my side I am able to face the world again. My wife was picked up and put in jail, leaving me with six children all under six to care for. I was ready to do something awful myself until one Saturday night I happened to listen to you and I let my Lord into my heart. From then on I have had the strength to carry on. In ninety days my wife will be home. She also has been converted."

From Northridge, California . . . "A man and wife that worked at my shop were saved the first night they saw you on TV. They were separating and breaking up their home. They had gone to the depot to buy a ticket for her to go to her folks in the east. God had other plans though. They missed the train and went back home to wait another day. However, at the urging of a fellow-worker he turned on your broadcast and when you asked the audience to accept Christ, they did so. They were so thrilled they went out and called the man that had asked them to listen to you and thanked him for it. He is now attending a good Bible preaching church and he and his wife have a bright future all because of your television broadcast."

From Lawrence, Kansas . . . "Last Saturday night my husband and I got down on our knees when you told us to. That is the first time I have ever seen my husband kneel."

From Detroit, Michigan . . . "Our ten year old boy who recently accepted Christ watched and listened with eagerness. Last week he said, 'I like the way Billy Graham explains everything.' Today the boys played ball and I could hardly get them in long enough to eat, but at five minutes to seven my son rushed in and put the TV on and without thinking I said, 'Which are you watching, Como or Gleason?' And I wish I could have a picture of his shining eyes when he said, 'Billy Graham.'"

From Florence, Mississippi . . . "During the end of your sermon something happened in my heart. I have been having so many problems but all of them went away then. I am nine years old."

From Magnetic Springs, Ohio . . . "I just finished listening to your program and wanted to write and tell you that I have accepted God as my Savior. I am twenty-one and have been completely paralyzed since I was eighteen. I am at a hospital where

18

they are helping me to adjust myself. When you ask for the people to come forward to accept God, my soul came too. Even lying in bed with my eyes closed I could feel the power of God within me."

From Perkasie, Pennsylvania . . . "I want to thank you for helping me. I am a girl nineteen and it seemed that for the past few years I have been falling deeper and deeper into depressing moods feeling that I had no reason to live on. You have opened my eyes to realize I have a reason—Jesus. I've been praying for a long, long time to find God and myself. With your help I have found Him. My heart feels new and at peace. I no longer feel alone because I know He is always with me."

From Bethlehem, Pennsylvania . . . "As I was watching you give the message of God on television Saturday night, I was also making a tape recording on my recorder for my brother-in-law who works nights and cannot watch. Well, it turned out that I made a recording that gave me a new life. I gave my heart to Christ."

What had happened? What reasonable explanation could account for such testimonies?

The New York Crusade was a mighty, co-operative effort between hundreds of churches and thousands of laymen and ministers and an inspired team of tireless evangelists headed by Billy Graham.

Working together, they made it possible for Graham to name these specific results:

First, New York has been confronted with the claims of Jesus Christ. This city has talked religion as perhaps not in several generations.

Second, the churches have a new vision of their great opportunities and responsibilities.

Third, there is a new unity among the churches.

Fourth, thousands of people have been transformed by the power of Christ.

Fifth, Christians have made new commitments to Christ.

Sixth, the crusade has stimulated a new surge of spiritual interest across the country.

Already the mail was bringing some positive evidence. Straws in the wind, perhaps!

"My cup runneth over," a mother wrote Graham from Staten Island. "I have been praying that my family might come to Christ. Thanks be to God, this wonderful miracle has happened. On June 2, my two children made their commitment. On June 12, my husband came to know Christ, too. This morning, my dear mother phoned and told me she was at the Garden last evening and went forward and is now truly a child of God.

"Our church has certainly felt the impact of this crusade by spiritual growth in each family that has attended and participated. Our minister seems to be growing in Christ too, and we are hearing the Gospel as never before preached from our pulpit. The little street I live on has experienced changes—people are talking 'Christ crucified'—and to date six people have made their commitment to Christ."

What had happened? Billy Graham had the answer.

"This has been God's doing, and it is marvelous in our eyes," he said. "Don't give the credit to me. Don't give it to our team. Don't give it to the churches even. Give it to God, where it belongs."

2

It is also a story about evangelist Billy Graham, who, before the crusade's start, wrote, "I feel inadequate and helpless. I go to New York in fear and trembling . . ."

Several hundred years before the birth of Jesus Christ, an ancient Hebrew prophet named Joel spoke thus: "And it shall come to pass afterward, that I will pour out my spirit upon all flesh; and your sons and daughters shall prophesy, your old men shall dream dreams, your young men shall see visions."

Since that day, it has been given to many young men to see visions of nations and races united in worship of Joel's God

20

through his son, Jesus Christ. One of these is the remarkable Dr. Billy Graham, of Montreat, North Carolina.

Billy Graham was born on a dairy farm on November 7, 1918.

He was converted at an evangelistic mission in Charlotte, North Carolina, when he was seventeen years old.

A stormy, self-conscious youth, he gradually matured into a serious-minded Bible-school student who first attracted public attention in Florida missions and Georgia arbor meetings as a boy evangelist.

After graduating from Wheaton College in Illinois, he served one brief pastorate at the nearby Western Springs Village Church, and then became executive vice-president for Youth for Christ International, in which organization his flair for evangelism led him through a series of crusade successes in the United States, Europe, India, and Asia.

In 1949 he conducted a crusade in Los Angeles that marked the beginning of his national prominence. After that date, as has been chronicled by magazines and newspapers, he marched from city to city and continent to continent in a crescendo of triumphs.

In the tradition of mass evangelism, he employed a team of increasingly capable assistants to bear part of the campaign burden, as did such celebrated revivalists as John Wesley, Moody and Sankey, and Dr. Billy Sunday.

In each city, they demonstrated an uncanny multiplication of skills in using the techniques of modern mass communications to create a growing audience.

Though his team of assistants expanded from one to twenty-one, and though his advertising budget zoomed from a two-dollar newspaper ad to a million-dollar television network, Billy Graham remained unchanged in at least two significant details.

First, he continued to preach the same Gospel.

Long ago he said, "I believe in the inspiration of the Holy Bible, the Virgin Birth, the resurrection of the Christ from the grave, the atonement by His blood of the sins of mankind, and the return of Christ to establish a kingdom on earth."

Second, he continued to regard his work as a holy mission and himself merely as God's ambassador, with no credit due him personally.

For years critics have hammered at what they called high-powered salesmanship. Some theologians have decried the superficiality of his doctrine. But no man has impugned his integrity.

Dr. Ralph Sockman, pastor of Christ Church on wealthy Park Avenue in New York, says, "The big thing about Billy Graham is that nobody—but nobody—laughs at him."

Rajkumari Amrit Kaur, India's minister of health, says, "Billy Graham is one of those rare jewels who tread this earth periodically and draw, by their lives and teaching, millions of others closer to God."

Stanley High, of the *Reader's Digest*, says, "His contagious sincerity and humility do not explain Billy Graham. Instead, they bring us to the conclusion that, in explaining him, something more than ordinary facts is involved."

What manner of man is he who has delivered God's message to more people than any other human in recorded history? What is the Pied Piper wizardry that has led forward the largest army of Christian converts since that day of Pentecost when Saint Peter preached to the men of Judea and with many words testified and exhorted until "they that gladly received his word were baptized, and the same day there were added unto them about three thousand souls?"

When the author told Graham at the start of the New York campaign that he expected to write a short history of the crusade, the evangelist generously volunteered the use of his personal diary. When it proved to be a better mirror of the man and his way of life than any outsider's statement, permission was asked and obtained to reproduce extended extracts from it.

Here is the first entry dealing with New York, written on May 9, six days before the initial meeting.

"This is one of those beautiful May mornings that makes one dislike being inside. This is the first spring that I have ever spent at home. Usually our campaigns have taken us in other places at this period of the year. I never dreamed the Blue Ridge Mountains could be so beautiful—dogwoods gleaming white, violets peeking up everywhere. What a wonderful and thrilling few weeks this has been: to run and play with my children every day, to listen to their little problems; to bow our knees and hearts together in the evening and offer our praises, worship and intercession to the Lord whom we all love; to tramp the woods with my two big dogs, Belshazzar and Princess; to visit a few neighbors in the community; to spend hours in my study every day with the Bible—these have been unforgettable days of preparation for the forthcoming New York Crusade.

"During the past few months we have faced many obstacles and problems. I guess I have been on the phone to New York an average of three or four times a day. Many problems seemed to be impossible to solve, and yet somehow they have been solved. It seemed a few months ago that opposition from the extreme liberals and the extreme fundamentalists would combine to put a hurdle in the pathway of blessing. Most of this opposition has now dissipated, I believe, in answer to prayer.

"My own attitude toward opposition has been one of quiet commitment to Christ. There were a few times, when I would hear some of the lies, distortions of truth and slander, that I had a bit of resentment in my heart and was tempted once or twice to lash back. But then scores of Scriptures began to echo in my ears and penetrate my heart, such as I Peter 2:15: 'For so is the will of God, that with well doing ye may put to silence the ignorance of foolish men.'

"Down in my heart I gradually began to give the opposition the benefit of the doubt. Most of their suppositions were based on ignorance of the true facts. I sensed the still small voice saying that in the end we would be vindicated.

"Gradually the Spirit of God shed abroad in my heart an overwhelming love for these brethren whom I believe to be tragically mistaken. I have thanked God a thousand times in the last few days that He gave me grace, during these months of severe attacks, never to answer back. I do not want to get my mind off Christ. We have been promised that if we keep our minds on Him the peace that passeth understanding will prevail in our hearts. This has certainly been true.

"The past few weeks have been weeks of filling up. The more I read and studied, it seemed, the less I knew, until today I feel more inadequate and helpless as I go to New York than at any time yet. I have a certain fear and dread, coupled with anticipation, as I board the train this afternoon for Washington and New York. New York is such a gigantic city, the opportunity and responsibility is overwhelming.

"The eyes of the entire Christian world will be on the New York Crusade. So much has been said and written, so much comment has been made, so much interest has been created throughout the world that whatever happens in this crusade will be discussed, prayed about, and even debated.

"I am now convinced that the Holy Spirit is going to answer the prayers of millions. My desk has been flooded daily with letters from all over the world informing me of the thrilling experiences that Christians are having everywhere praying for the New York Crusade. I have received letters from over forty-five countries, some of them unbelievable letters of people praying many times all night that God would send a spiritual awakening to New York City. I believe that in His own way God will answer those multiplied prayers.

"I heard about one prayer meeting where the women gathered —there were divisions among them, some were not speaking to each other; before the meeting was over, they were in each other's arms, their tears mingling together as their hearts were united by the Holy Spirit. One dear little Chinese lady from behind the Iron Curtain came into Hong Kong, attended one of the prayer meetings, and gave her bracelet to be sent to the New York committee to help them with their finances. A prayer meeting in Europe ended up with five being converted. A prayer meeting in Singapore, with scores present, had many conversions before it ended. As a New York pastor recently said, 'If the meetings are never held, it will have been worth the tremendous spirit of expectancy that has been created among Christians all over the world.'

"As I go to New York, I go with a thankful heart for the past few weeks that I have had the privilege of drawing myself apart. I told Ruth yesterday that I could not recall in the last few years when I had felt so well physically. She said, 'Darling, it is in answer to the prayers of people everywhere.' I had a strange feeling that she was right. During the month of April it was 'prayer month' all over the world. Those prayers have been gathering in momentum and intensity. I am beginning to feel these prayers.

"Physically I have never felt so well. Spiritually I sense the presence of God. Sermon outlines and thoughts have been coming to my mind and heart as few other times in my ministry. I am convinced that the concentration of prayers is moving the hand of God. I sensed this same thing in London three years ago and again in India last year. I know that we are going to one of the strongholds of Satan. Materialism, indifference and wickedness are apparent to even a casual Christian observer in New York. The church is receding and losing ground. We have found many of the ministers to be discouraged and, in some cases, almost desperate. This great united spiritual crusade is going to ignite the wrath of Satan. All the forces of hell will probably be turned on us. If the climax of my ministry is to end in crucifixion, by God's grace I am ready. In fact, I count it a joy to be tried. It is a glorious challenge, it is a thrilling adventure to have the privilege, if necessary, to suffer and fight for Christ.

"There are many of my friends who have predicted that the New York Crusade would end in failure. From the human viewpoint and by human evaluation it may be a flop. However, I am convinced in answer to the prayers of millions that in the sight of God and by heaven's evaluation it will be no failure. God will have His way, and in some unknown and remarkable way Christ will receive the glory and honor.

"One of the things that has sickened me has been the concentration of publicity around my name. As quickly as possible this gaze on me and our team must be shifted to the Person of Christ. I must decrease and He must increase. I have expressed often that God will not share His glory with another. When any one man becomes the center of attention, he is in danger of eclipsing his ministry. Thank God for all interest that has been stirred among people everywhere, but it is my prayer that the interest will be focused in Christ.

"Today Ruth and I took our last stroll to see our four sheep and to lie on the grass, talking, quoting Scripture and praying together. What a wonderful companion she is—so full of Scripture for every occasion and every event. Certainly our marriage was formed and planned in heaven. I shall miss the children during the next few weeks. I have come to love this mountain top and would like nothing better than for the Lord to say that I should stay here the rest of my life. I do not naturally like to go out to the wars. It is so peaceful and restful here. But duty calls. I must put on the whole armor of God and go forth to meet the foe."

The foe of an evangelist is not always wholly apparent to a cheering populace. Traditionally, the man of God is expected to fight the devil, but there are also other enemies. A forgotten sage who must have met them all once wrote:

"An evangelist must be many things to many people. The

25

preacher for this work must have the heart of a lion, the patience of a donkey, the wisdom of an elephant, the industry of an ant, and as many lives as a cat."

In New York, the scene of Graham's greatest test, he would soon test the profundity of those words.

3 *In New York Graham's team and a host of volunteers were in training . . . 4000 for the choir, 5000 in counseling classes, and 3000 ushers for service in gigantic Madison Square Garden . . .*

One night after attending a preliminary meeting in New York City, Graham returned to his hotel room and wearily dropped onto the bed. Unable to get to sleep, he reached for his Bible. It fell open and his eyes fastened upon this verse in Ezekiel 24:

"Woe to the bloody city. I also will make the pile great. Heap on the logs, kindle the fire, boil well the flesh, and empty out the broth, and let the bones be burned up. Then set it empty upon the coals, that it may become hot, and its copper may burn, that its filthiness may be melted in it, its rust consumed. In vain I have wearied myself . . ."

To the evangelist this was a message from heaven. He could not resist making a phone call in the middle of the night to Jerry Beavan, his fellow team member, executive secretary, and public-relations man. "Listen to what I found," he cried. "Here's my message for New York."

This was not a recent concern. In 1947 he said, "America's greatest enemy is not the hammer and sickle. It is the internal decadence that is causing us to rush faster than any civilization before us toward destruction and hell."

More recently: "One of these days the dam is going to break and the waters are going to flood America. We will have no more America unless God can visit us with an old-fashioned, heaven-sent, Holy Ghost revival."

26

Always he knew that the nerve center of America was New York: that its citizens controlled the nation's business, industry, finance, art, culture, communications, etc. He knew, too, that almost 56 per cent of those people went to no church whatever; that sixty nationalities loved and hated and labored within its boundaries; that it had more Catholics than lived in Rome, and more Puerto Ricans than lived in San Juan—and four times as many Irish as lived in Dublin.

He knew that only a handful of Protestants, comparatively speaking, existed in that polyglot population. About 7.5 per cent of the whole population.

Once he confessed, "I have prayed, worried, and wept over New York more than any other place in which we have held a crusade. I sometimes stand in the middle of that great city and wonder if I can ever reach it for God."

Yet it had to be tackled. Graham has a fund of anecdotes which he sprinkles through his sermons. One favorite illustrates mankind's astonishing capability despite impossible odds.

"I heard about a fellow," he says, "who went home from work along a path through a cemetery. One night after dusk somebody had dug a new grave right across his pathway, and the poor fellow fell into it. Well, he tried to climb the sides, but they were too high. He pulled up roots and threw out clods and made an awful uproar, but nobody came to help him. Finally he made up his mind to go to sleep until morning.

"Well, along about midnight another man came down that path on his way to a coon hunt. And he fell into the grave. He tried to climb the walls, but they were too high and he pulled up roots and threw out clods and made a great uproar, but not a soul responded.

"Except one. As the coon hunter leaned back to get his breath, he felt a cold, clammy hand clutch his shoulder and he heard a deep voice say, 'You cain't get out of this grave, mister.'

"But he did!"

London had been a tough city for a crusade; so had Glasgow, New Orleans, and Boston. Critics had said he would fail. "Our people are different," they warned. "You can't win converts here."

But he did!

So now the opening service of the Billy Graham Crusade in

New York was only a week away. The Lord's battalions were assembling before the walls of modern Jericho.

Months earlier the preliminaries that must undergird every crusade had been completed.

The invitation to Graham had come from the Department of Evangelism of the Protestant Council of the City of New York, representing Council churches and other religious organizations.

An executive committee of prominent businessmen and clergymen had been appointed to sponsor and organize the crusade, raise the necessary funds, and supervise all expenditures. In point of fact, this was to be New York City's own crusade, not Graham's. These men, having met together with Jerry Beavan for months, now had approved a budget of $900,000 for six weeks, the largest appropriation in the history of evangelism.

Months earlier, Beavan had negotiated a contract for Madison Square Garden at rentals averaging approximately $28,000 per week. He had sought and obtained options for July and August as well, although no sensible man would predict that the crusade might run through the midsummer heat.

Assisted by other team members, he had arranged for an intense advertising program.

Other team members slipped quietly into town and settled down behind desks in Crusade Headquarters at 165 West Forty-sixth Street, where their windows were lighted at night by the Great White Way.

Mrs. Betty Lowry, press secretary, tried to meet the demands of newsmen for interviews and information with cheerful efficiency.

Prayer partners were recruited, almost 200,000 throughout the world, in more than 100 countries.

Churches and pastors were invited to co-operate, and 1500 responded.

Choristers were invited to sing in Cliff Barrows' giant choir, and 4000 responded.

Church workers were invited to attend a series of nine training classes which would equip them to counsel and guide those who responded to Graham's invitation, and 5000 responded.

Ushers were invited to volunteer for patrol duty in Garden corridors and aisles, and 3000 responded.

Volunteers were mailing out letters by the hundreds of thousands for scores of committee members. Prayer groups were meeting under the leadership of Mrs. Norman Vincent Peale in ten districts, which in turn were subdivided into hundreds of smaller zones.

Without anyone being aware of it, the crusade organization had suddenly burgeoned into a streamlined, expertly staffed, human organism.

And as happens in all crusades, the passing of time provided a few clinkers and a few "flaps."

One morning Graham's friends were astonished to read in the New York *Times* that "Graham Expects to End Crusades." The *Times* stated that the evangelist, in talking to some Episcopal clergymen, had said he could continue "certainly not too much longer." With telephones ringing wildly and Western Union messengers racing in and out, Graham's headquarters protested that he had been misunderstood.

Presently he made it official by writing an article for the *Christian Herald*. "I'm not quitting," he declared. "I am an evangelist because I cannot be otherwise. Humanly, there are other things which I would prefer to do; activities that would permit me to be with my children in the growing, crucial years, but inwardly, there is a still small voice saying, 'This is the Way; walk ye in it,' and so I must walk. . . . I will never quit until God takes His Hand off me or calls me home to heaven."

Then there was what insiders called the Cohen "flap."

Late in March, Graham received a phone call from Mickey Cohen, former Los Angeles gambling czar and underworld target. Graham had tried in vain to lead Cohen to Christ during his 1949 crusade in Los Angeles. Since then, Cohen had served time in a federal prison. His call pleaded for a meeting and Graham agreed. The result was unexpectedly heralded by a United Press story that said, "Mickey Cohen held a five hour prayer meeting and talk yesterday with Billy Graham in Cohen's Waldorf-Astoria suite. It was the dapper Cohen's first trip East since he got out of prison in 1955, and he said he made it to see his old friend, Graham.

"'I am very high on the Christian way of life,' said Cohen, now a respectable and wealthy greenhouse operator. 'I wish I could lead the kind of life Billy does.'

"Cohen continued, 'Billy came up and before we had food he said—what do you call it, that thing they say before the food—

grace! yeah, grace! Then we talked a lot about Christianity stuff. He stayed four or five hours.'"

Reporters scented a sensational conversion. They knew that Graham had helped other prominent people to find Christ as Savior. When they cornered the evangelist in Buffalo, where he was delivering an address, he said, "I have talked to Mr. Cohen on a number of occasions. On every occasion we talked about spiritual matters and about the possibility of receiving Christ as his Savior. Today, we had Bible reading and prayer together. This is something between me and the Lord and the other person. Almost weekly I conduct such private meetings with persons of news importance, but this is almost the only time such news has reached the newspapers. My job is to try to win every person to Christ, especially persons that would have influence for Christ in our society. Surely a man ought to be able to seek spiritual counsel without having his search publicized."

And that was that, except for Mickey's attendance at the Garden to hear Graham preach, which inspired another salvo of editorial conjectures.

April showers in New York also brought two surprising attacks. The first from the Reverend John E. Kelly, of the National Catholic Welfare Conference, was headlined in these words:

"Shun Graham Crusade, Priest Urges Catholics!"

Father Kelly, writing in a Catholic paper, had said that Graham was "a danger to the faith . . . So well constructed are his sermons, though interwoven with false and true doctrines, so forceful and persuasive is his delivery that even a fairly well-instructed Catholic may be deceived. He preaches many true doctrines but skips some essential ones, and thus provides at most a part-way guide to heaven. Billy's converts are only half-saved."

Then he added a pat on the back, saying that Graham "is certainly a man of prayer, humble, dedicated, devout. We should pray for Billy Graham."

The second attack came from a fundamentalist group, the American Council of Christian Churches, meeting in convention in Jacksonville, Florida. Their inhospitable resolution said:

"Dr. Graham, in his effort to attract all groups . . . has pursued a course which this Council, committed as it is to the historic Protestant faith, must warn people against. The principle of compromising God's commands that souls be saved is nothing more than doing evil that good may come, and it never does. The New York meeting in the end will do untold harm to the cause of evangelical Christianity. This Council cannot endorse Dr. Graham's New York campaign . . ."

On the positive side, a number of significant stories began to reach the public. In April the New York *Times* magazine summarized, for its influential readership, Graham's interpretation of his role as an evangelist.

"'The meaning of the word "evangelist" is proclaimer, a proclaimer of good news,'" the article quoted Graham. "'My job is simply to proclaim the Gospel, and to let the Spirit of God apply in the individual hearts.'

"'There will be no emotional outbursts at Madison Square Garden,' Graham promised. 'When I give the invitation for people to receive Christ it will be so quiet you can hear a pin drop. It will be as holy and reverent a moment as any you would have in any church in the worship service. And you will see people coming forward deliberately, quietly, reverently, thoughtfully, and many of their lives—the evidence will pile up for years to come—will have been transformed and changed in that moment.'

"He preaches an elementary, 'hard' Gospel of sin and salvation," the *Times* said.

On Easter Sunday, through *This Week* magazine, he told "Why New York is My Greatest Challenge." "I have been concerned about New York for years," he wrote. "Because of its size and its importance in the cultural and communications fields, New York has a special influence on the rest of the country and even on the whole world. A spiritual awakening in New York could echo all over the world.

"New York has enormous spiritual potentiality. It is an exciting city in the energy of its people. What must be done is to take the emphasis off evil and change men by the new birth which Christ offers by his death and resurrection. This Gospel message could transform New York.

"Just 100 years ago . . . a few businessmen met in the North Dutch Church on Fulton Street to pray for a spiritual revival in America. The number grew until 10,000 people were praying daily for a religious awakening. This resulted in a revival that added over a million people to the churches of America in one year.

"We would like to see this happen again."

By the second Saturday in May, metropolitan New York was ready to welcome—or reject, perhaps—the man who, according to the careless manner of writing of some reporters, was coming to "save" New York:

It was ready with 650 twenty-four-sheet billboards posted at strategic locations within the Greater New York area.

It was ready with 40,000 phone dials reading "Pray for Billy Graham"; 40,000 bumper strips; 250,000 crusade songbooks; 100,000 Gospels of Saint John; 1,000,000 letterheads; 2,500,000 envelope stuffers; and 35,000 window posters.

Nobody in all history had conceived a crusade so mighty as this joint production of the evangelist, his team, the 1500 churches that were his hosts, and Almighty God.

Checking last-minute details, a team member visited the Garden and returned to headquarters with a haggard expression. "Those circus animals," he said. "I wish they'd get them out of the Garden."

"They'll be out—three days ahead of the crusade."

"But that smell," the young man said. "The circus stables are where we'll be holding our prayer meetings. Whew!"

Down South, Billy Graham was writing in his diary, "I go to New York in fear and trembling."

4   *Going north, Graham paused to visit a friend in the White House, then raced on to answer reporters who asked, why are you here, what is your goal?*

On the mountain where Graham lives in North Carolina, he has a secret place to which he retires when he seeks communion with his Maker. Before his trip north, he spent many hours within its reassuring borders.

The imminence of the New York Crusade, and its significance, were always heavy in his meditations. New York was a unique responsibility. To the Christian in Katako Kombe, Central Africa, or Kabul, Afghanistan, or Conchillas, Uruguay, New York might seem to be another place, another world. And yet, unbeknown to him, what happened there could leave its mark on him. Billy Graham knew this. He had traveled much of God's earth, from Paris to Formosa, Manila to Berlin, and understood better than most that the entire globe watched New York City and, perhaps, might follow its guidance.

Jesus had commissioned his disciples: "Ye shall be witnesses unto Me both in Jerusalem, and in all Judea, and in Samaria, and unto the uttermost part of the earth." Those words were Billy Graham's marching orders; he must soon play David to New York's Goliath. And as the uncertainty of a world with its intercontinental missiles and hydrogen-bomb warheads increased, so did the urgency of his crusade.

But what would his welcome be? Would this be God's hour for New York? Billy Graham remembered the brassy two-page splash published in the New York *Sunday Mirror* in early spring. Under a headline, "Beat the Devil out of New York," Elizabeth Bussing had said, "The brash, blasé big town stands ready to be jolted from the Battery to the Bronx as Evangelist Billy Graham squares off against Sin in the world's most unhallowed battleground, Madison Square Garden. The bell sounds May 15th in a six weeks' knock-em-down and drag-em-out fight to the finish."

This was surely an unseemly heralding of the Lord's evangelist, but yet it was a part of what an evangelist must learn to expect. What Graham had not expected when he left his home in Montreat en route to his train was the lump in his throat and the tear in his eye. As he wrote in his diary, taking leave of his little family tugged at his heart. He wrote, "I had enjoyed being home more than during any other period of my ministry. During the past few months I have been home more than at any other time. I had gotten to know my children . . . My little boy, Franklin, kept saying, 'Daddy, don't go.' Or, 'Daddy, why don't you stay with us?' The two older girls Gigi and Anne, understand. They have already given their hearts and their lives to Christ. They were glad for me to go, and both of them told me before I left that they would be praying for me. Little Bunny said that she remembered me in

33

prayer every day. They'll never know what their little child-like prayers on my behalf mean to me."

When Graham got on the train, it was not to go directly to New York but first to pay a call on an old friend, President Eisenhower. He wrote about his May 10 visit thus:

". . . I went directly to the President's office. He was standing up, and he said, 'Hello there, my friend.' I'm always impressed with President Eisenhower's freshness and alertness. During my visits with him our conversations have usually been on spiritual matters. Sometimes they have digressed to the race problem, foreign policy, his farm at Gettysburg, or golf; but mostly they are about moral and spiritual matters.

"I reviewed for the President the plans for the New York Crusade. I could tell that he had already read a great deal about it . . . He said it would be a wonderful thing if people all over the world could love each other. I agreed, and I tried to point out that the Gospel has a vertical as well as a horizontal aspect, that men must be born again and be truly converted to Christ before they have the capacity to love. He heartily agreed.

"I have always made it a policy never to quote the President, so the newspaper men get very little out of me after I talk with the President . . . Whatever celebrity I talk to, I try to keep his conversation in confidence. Therefore, I have never revealed my private conversations with the outstanding people that it has been my privilege to meet. I make one point clear, however, and that is—whoever I go to see—I am there as a representative of Christ. I am His ambassador, representing Him, and I always pray for an opportunity to witness for Him."

The morning after his visit with Eisenhower, Billy Graham roused, as the dawn was breaking, to join his wife Ruth on the through train to New York City. Together they would arrive; together they would later make their first public appearance at a press conference. Now, though, there was a wait in the chilly early morn, for the train was an hour late.

At last, however, Billy Graham wrote, "I was on board car SR-44. The porter was an old friend of mine who had just had a heart attack. He is a dear man of God and is always such a blessing. Ruth was awake and said she hadn't been able to sleep since two o'clock. I went immediately to bed and was soon sound asleep,

34

waking about nine when Paul Maddox brought some toast and coffee to our room. It tasted wonderful."

As the train was approaching New York, Billy's heart became "more burdened and more concerned. I began to ask myself, 'Would God send a revival into New York or was this going to be a complete flop as many had predicted.' As my heart agonized and I began to pray, a sweet and wonderful assurance came over me that this was God's hour, that we were in the Will of God, and that He was going to do a great and mighty thing in this city."

When they arrived in New York—still late—a score of old friends were there to greet him. (As were twenty-five press photographers.) It was a strange feeling at first, the absence of pushing crowds, of hymns filling the air, of backslapping hands. In London and Glasgow thousands of good people had stormed into the railway stations and welcomed him like a home-town hero. New York sent only newsmen and a handful of friends. He must have wondered, was this an augury?

Then he and Ruth walked through the subway tunnel that leads under Manhattan's asphalt like a gigantic mole run. As flash bulbs popped, the little people of the big town began to take notice.

"God bless you, Billy!" one shouted.

Another grabbed him and whispered in his ear, "We sure need you here."

"It seemed to be a harbinger and a foretaste of what was to come," he wrote.

After several years of experience Graham remains apprehensive of the institution of the press conference. "I always face the press with fear, anxiety, and complete dependence upon the Lord," he says. "I think I pray about a press conference more than I do about my sermons. It is so easy to put one word in the wrong place, or to say a sentence that someone can misunderstand. It is so easy to be misquoted and misinterpreted."

As he strode swiftly into the conference room at the New Yorker Hotel and faced scores of newsmen and women who had been waiting for over an hour, he saw the usual challenging, noncommittal faces of professional journalists. What would they do to him on this morning of May 11?

He remembered London and its initial barrage of verbal garbage. That had been his worst experience. There a columnist had

35

charged that Graham accused England of being frustrated, disillusioned, and on the verge of being destroyed by its socialistic government. "It's a foul lie," the reporter screamed in type. "Apologize or stay away!"

Another wrote, without ever having seen him, "In action, Billy Graham uses the Bible like an anvil. He pounds it. He clouts it. He belts it. It seems a pity that we haven't got a bigger load of native devilment for Billy to sort out, and London seems such a poor sort of Sodom and Gomorrah for such a fervid, cleansing talent."

The Communist press said flatly, "Billy Graham, go home!"

But the New York reception was altogether different. Now, not only had Graham's genuine humility and sincerity won over many of his severest detractors, but his knowledge of men had deepened.

The hundred reporters who had been waiting seemed friendly and patient. "How different," Graham wrote in his diary, "from the first London news conference three years ago. There seemed to be no trick questions, and as I looked into their faces, very little skepticism . . . I pity some reporters who have never been to evangelistic services who are assigned to cover an evangelist. It would be as if I were asked to go to a football game and cover it, having never seen a football game—I am sure that what I would write in the press the next day would be distorted. The miracle is not that there are misquotes, but that there are not more of them. We should thank God that here in America the press has changed its attitude and is now so friendly to religion, whereas a few years ago it more or less ignored religion."

The atmosphere of the press conference was cordial. The reporters had been given ten pages of questions and Graham's answers about the New York Crusade, prepared in advance. Generally the reporters seemed satisfied with the material; none was ostensibly skeptical or cynical. Several thoughtful questions were asked. Why, one reporter wondered, was a revival needed when the membership in the churches was zooming? Graham's answer: "This is a time of great religious inquiry, attested by huge church memberships. But one must get down to the level of the individual. Figures are no good unless religious morality gets down to the personal lives of the people."

Audiences of 19,000 faced Dr. Billy Graham night after night in Madison Square Garden. His New York Crusade ran longer and attracted more people than any religious campaign in history. More than 2,000,000 people heard him in the Garden and at outside rallies. More than 56,000 made decisions for Christ. Of these, 20,000 were teen-agers. An estimated 96,000,000 saw this Garden scene on television. Total cost of this most successful of all Graham's crusades was approximately $2,500,000.

At the end of each sermon Graham invited his hearers to come forward and accept Christ. "I'm going to ask you to come," he said. "Come quickly, right now. Get up out of your seats from all over, quietly and reverently, and come stand here for a moment. If you are with friends or relatives, they will wait. Don't let distance keep you from Christ. Christ went to the Cross because He loved you. Certainly you can come these few steps. Come right now. Come while the choir sings. Christians, you pray!" And the people came, more than 56,000.

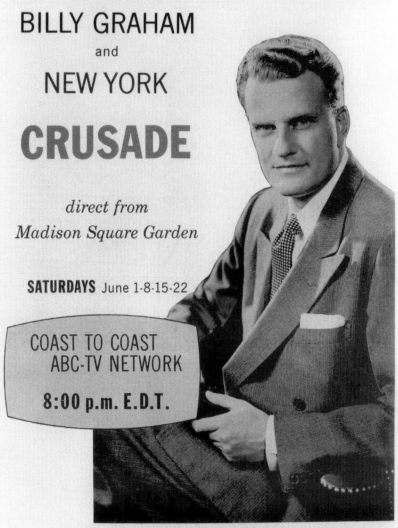

ON TELEVISION

BILLY GRAHAM
and
NEW YORK

CRUSADE

direct from
Madison Square Garden

SATURDAYS June 1-8-15-22

COAST TO COAST
ABC-TV NETWORK

8:00 p.m. E.D.T.

see your newspaper for local time and station

Beginning June 1, 1957, the American Broadcasting Company network made a prime-time hour available each Saturday night. For the first time, Americans who had heard of Billy Graham were able to see a crusade and hear the Gospel in the comfort of their living rooms. The initial schedule of four weekly telecasts was extended to 17 programs broadcast from Madison Square Garden.

Asked about segregation, Graham answered, "There is no segregation at the foot of the Cross . . ."

Another reporter wanted to know if it was a criticism of the church today that people respond to him as an evangelist and not to the churches themselves. "Yes and no," Billy said. "Evangelism is the fire truck of the church. When the fire truck comes along, all other vehicles get out of the way, and when the fire truck has done its job, the other vehicles begin to run again."

One of the most provocative queries was about sin and New York. A reporter charged Graham with saying that New York was a wicked town. "How sinful do you think New York is? Is it worse than other cities in the world?" Graham's answer: no. "What I have said is that whatever condition does exist here exists because there is more of New York than there is of any other city in the world. If there is more sin in New York, it is because there are more people."

Finally the conference was over. For a few moments there would be enough time to join Ruth and Roger Hull, chairman of the crusade executive committee, for an afternoon lunch. Then the phone began to ring.

"I must speak to Dr. Graham immediately. . . ."

"Dr. Graham, please. This is urgent!"

For four months such calls would come every hour of the day and night, from friends, contributors, editors, reporters, photographers, politicians, lost souls, alcoholics, neurotics, and scalawags.

This was the beginning of the hardest part of every crusade. "My wife and I have lost our privacy," he told a reporter. "And I don't think anyone who has lost their privacy doesn't long to have it back. You don't realize what a priceless possession it is to be a private individual. To be looked at, to be stared at everywhere one goes, never to go into a restaurant without being looked at . . ."

He took some calls and his helpers answered the others. Magazines wanted exclusive interviews and photo stories, and so did newspapers and press associations. TV and radio producers stood in line to seek his personal appearance. Clubs invited him to speak at lunches. To Graham, it was all religious work. Later, four days later, he would preach. Now he must show the Lord's colors to the vast unchurched multitude.

5   *That first, frantic week, Graham was a willing puppet pulled by the strings of his ministry, at beck and call of press, TV, and radio, to the end that the whole people should hear and read of his crusade . . .*

In 1949 a baffled editor of a paper in Los Angeles read a telegram over and over. It contained only the two words, "Puff Graham," and it was signed by his boss, William Randolph Hearst.

"You know any Grahams?" he asked an assistant.

"There's a young evangelist with that name preaching in a tent downtown."

"What's he got that's so good?"

The newspaperman said, "He's got looks. He's got personality. He ought to be in pictures."

"Get some photographers and feature writers," the editor ordered. "Go out and give him the treatment."

That was the year that Graham began to learn the benefits of publicity.

His diary is a revelation of the drudgery of this aspect of his evangelistic campaigns, and his selfless contribution to it.

"It is strange how one has gotten used to publicity," he once wrote. "I used to so terribly resent the invasion of our privacy; now we have learned to live with it and have dedicated it many times to the Lord. I realize that the same press that has made us known could ruin us overnight. I also realize that the crowds that applauded Christ on Palm Sunday crucified Him on Friday. The masses of people are fickle, therefore I have learned to put my trust in God, who is unmovable and who never changes, so that when the day of crucifixion and suffering comes to me I will be unmoved."

But could he do enough, he wondered? In a city teeming with people whose exteriors had become case-hardened by the struggle for survival, was there any chink through which he could penetrate their armor with God's message?

This next week was the critical time. These were the critical days. Long ago he had learned that editors wanted only news and controversy. No evangelist makes news when he sits in a hotel room. Somehow, the public had to realize that a great thing was going to happen, that God was perhaps about to visit Madison Square Garden.

They had to be persuaded to visit the Garden, instead of the races, theater, movies, night ball games, and instead of sitting in slippered ease before a TV spectacular. No other evangelist ever faced such high-powered competition.

The only weapon at hand to use against New York's colossal indifference was one with two legs, a voice, a message and—fortunately—wavy hair and a good profile. No walking around this city's walls seven times to make them collapse. This was a job for a battering ram, a job for nothing less than God's own word.

Four days before the first Garden service, he wrote:

"I went over to the office to meet Walter Cronkite, who was going to do a film to be used on CBS Television. I had met Walter before and appeared on one of his shows. He is a keen analyst and an excellent, amiable host. We had a great time making the program.

"On the way back to the hotel, met *Look* magazine's David Zing, writer, and a young man named Bob, photographer. Dave had covered us before. We went down and had a hot dog at one of the little hot dog places along Times Square. People began gathering around, wanting autographs, and saying, 'God bless you, Billy.' 'We're for you, Billy!' etc.

"It is quite amazing that a preacher can walk down Times Square and be recognized. Some people grip your hand as though they would like to have a talk. There seems to be a spiritual hunger settling upon people in the city. It is something I have never quite felt in any other place."

On Sunday there was another TV program, Steve Allen's.

"I had some hesitancy about taking this engagement because the Steve Allen Show is a variety show. However, I remembered that Jesus ate with publicans and sinners even though He was denounced by the Pharisees. Here was an opportunity to give my testimony to forty million Americans over NBC Television.

39

"The first person I ran into was Tallulah Bankhead; she grabbed my hand and said, 'I've been looking forward to meeting you for a long time.' She was extremely warm and cordial, urging Ruth and me to come over to her apartment for tea sometime.

"The next person I saw was Milton Berle. Then Pearl Bailey came up and shook my hand and said that her father was a minister and that she was looking forward to attending the meetings. She indicated that God was her agent and that she believed in prayer and the Bible.

"I talked to all of them several times and became conscious that all of these people were also searching for some reality in life. The floor director squeezed my arm and said, 'God bless you. I'm a Christian, too. See you Wednesday night.' Here the Lord had His witness right in the heart of one of the great variety shows on television.

"Before going on the show I was a bit nervous. I don't get before that many people every day; but I also had a quiet confidence that God was with us. On the program I felt completely relaxed and at home and believe the Lord helped us to get across a testimony."

One columnist has charged that Graham carries a corps of press agents with him. This is completely untrue. One young woman, Mrs. Betty Lowry, aided by one full-time assistant, was his entire press staff. Jerry Beavan handled all radio and TV commitments, in addition to many other duties. Even a one-ring circus would have hired many more bell ringers.

Graham's publicity originates with editors and producers. They go to him, not he to them. The Allen show is an example of how the system works. A newsman who had written often about Graham happened to be talking to Steve in the spring of 1957. "You ought to get Graham when he comes to town," he suggested. "How can I reach him?" Allen demanded. "Try calling Jerry Beavan at Crusade Headquarters."

Minutes later, Beavan picked up his phone. "This is Steve Allen," a voice said. "I'd like to invite Billy to be my guest the Sunday before the crusade starts. Will he consider it?"

Beavan said, "I think it can be arranged."

It was as simple as that, even including the phone call from Allen's business manager that followed Graham's acceptance. He wanted to pay Billy a fee, but the answer was "No." He then said,

"We'd like to contribute something to his work. Would that be okay?"

It would, and they did, a check for fifteen hundred dollars.

His diary for Monday said, "This morning I was on the Bill Leonard Show, which is called, 'This is New York.' They made five programs to use each day this week. At eleven o'clock I was on with John Cameron Swayze on ABC-TV. At two o'clock I had a very interesting interview with the famous New York *Mirror* columnist, Sidney Field. He is one of the most unusual, fascinating and penetrating columnists that I have talked to in a long time."

Then—"Tuesday morning I was with Martha Dean on her show at WOR. She was a very interesting radio interviewer and newscaster. Her sponsor is the New York *Times*. I felt that the questions she asked me indicated a genuine personal interest. She kept me on for forty-five minutes, asking the most penetrating and interesting questions.

"At twelve noon, Ruth and I arrived at the Waldorf-Astoria Hotel where we were to be interviewed by Tex and Jinx McCrary, on coast-to-coast NBC-TV. This was an interesting experience. We fell in love with Tex and Jinx. They were so warm and friendly and made us feel at home right away. They practically gave us their show and at the end allowed me to preach a message to the thousands of people who must have been viewing."

In the meantime, New York newspapers had not been idle. After announcing his arrival, however, there was little immediate stuff for headlines. News columnist Danton Walker reported that "a national magazine had tried to get Graham to write a piece naming the ten most corrupt spots in New York. He declined."

Hearst columnist George Sokolsky published an invidious comparison between Graham's complicated preparations and "the simplicity of Saint Paul's organization that nevertheless succeeded in converting the entire world."

The Hearst-owned *American Weekly* magazine gave its ten million-plus families Graham's own by-lined story of what he thought about American morals. He thought many of our troubles stemmed from taking "God out of our educational system and the Bible out of our schools." Citing a famous survey, he said, "Did you know that only one divorce in fifty-seven marriages took place where the family went to church regularly? And did you know that there was only one divorce out of five hundred marriages where there is daily Bible study and prayer in the home?"

Tuesday afternoon he had a foretaste of things to come when he spoke at the service dedicating Madison Square Garden to the service of the Lord.

"We could only have the Garden forty-five minutes," he wrote. "A show was ending its rehearsal about five-thirty and would be opening about seven-thirty, so we had to be brief. I went to the Garden Club and met with various members of the Committee and Team. Then we went on the platform about six-ten.

"Already about five or six thousand people had gathered. These were the counselors, ushers, choir members, and ministers. One could almost sense the presence of God. I gave a brief message on Paul's readiness to go to Rome when he said, 'I am a debtor . . . I am ready . . . I am unashamed.' The associate evangelists were introduced—and what a fine-looking group of dedicated ministers of the Gospel they were! Any denomination would be proud to have them as ministers. I am certain, as Dr. Paul Rees led in a moving prayer of dedication, that heaven must have smiled. We could sense the presence of God.

"At the end of the service, I asked people who would rededicate their lives to God to stand up, and *the whole congregation stood;* with the exception of only a few who were largely newspaper people."

But the end was not yet. So gracious a person as Billy Graham finds it difficult to resist even the less reasonable requests of journalists. Now the dedication service was over. It was dusk, a time for relaxing. He wrote:

"Came back to the hotel. My original plans for the evening had been to visit as many of the all-night prayer meetings as possible, but due to fatigue I had thought it best to go to bed and get as much rest as possible. The next day being our opening, it might be very strenuous. I returned to the room and Cornell Capa and Dick Billings of *Life* magazine came in. They felt that they must have some more pictures for their story. We had quite a discussion about the type of pictures, and finally, since it was raining, and they thought it would make good pictures, I consented to take a walk through Times Square.

"We walked along the Great White Way while they were snapping pictures. I spoke to a number of people, encouraging every one to come to the meetings; spoke to a few about Christ.

"We walked over to Calvary Baptist Church. Standing in front were a number of photographers from *Look* magazine and *Match* magazine. A reporter and photographer had flown over from Paris to represent *Match* in covering the first few nights of the meetings. *Match* is the *Life* magazine of France and they have carried stories on our work in Britain and in Paris. I also met reporters from Sweden, Holland and Australia. The interest in other parts of the world is beyond all our expectation.

"I spoke briefly to the congregation at Calvary Baptist Church. There were about five hundred people in prayer. How thrilling it was to see so many people at that time of night planning to spend all night. We have received telegrams and letters from all over the world indicating that all-night prayer meetings are being held in many countries tonight. Certainly God is going to answer the prayers of so many people."

And finally—May 15—*der Tag!* The Day!

At the crack of dawn Graham beavered away to Dave Garroway's crack-of-dawn telecast called "Today."

"When I walked in, Gloria Swanson met me," he wrote. "She, too, was a guest on the program, and we had about half an hour of intense discussion. She seems to be a dedicated woman who is deeply concerned about the moral problems of America. She is dedicating her life to helping clean up the country. I hadn't been with her long until I realized that America would be a wonderful place if more of our film stars were like Gloria Swanson. I invited her to the meetings and she promised to come.

"Dave Garroway asked some wonderful leading questions that allowed me to preach the Gospel. Then, outside the NBC studios, I made another television program for NBC. What a glorious and thrilling opportunity to present the Gospel. It is difficult for me to understand how some of the religious critics could point their fingers of skepticism; even if my methods are less than perfect and if they consider them all wrong, they should rejoice that opportunities are being given to preach the Gospel on television, radio, through newspapers and secular magazines. When have we seen such opportunities in our generation? It should cause all Christians to rejoice. It has greatly humbled me."

That afternoon there were a few minutes only for a fast review

43

of events. Things seemingly were shipshape. During the week, a meeting with the finance committee had indicated that money for the crusade was coming in at a rate only slightly less than satisfactory. One generous Christian had even guaranteed a hundred thousand dollars toward a series of network TV broadcasts of the services.

Team members were returning from all-night prayer meetings to resume their daytime chores. All their affairs seemed in order. Tonight's delegations would occupy seven thousand seats, delivered to the Garden, most of them, in 114 busses, which would be parked, by special police permission, between Forty-second and Fifty-seventh streets on Ninth Avenue, the longest bus stop in the world.

Some argument had attended the assignment of seats to church delegations. If pastors and congregations were interested enough to write in advance—sometimes weeks ahead—it seemed logical to give them the best main-floor seats. Other voices expressed the long-time Graham philosophy:

"We are here to give God's message to the *unchurched*. Let them have the choice seats, first come first served. Let the church delegations praise the Lord from our balconies."

Once, a very important minister asked Graham to address an important convention assembly in a nearby city. "Come talk to us," he said. "I'll guarantee there'll be ten thousand preachers there."

Graham said, "Preachers don't need me. But if you'll guarantee an audience of ten thousand sinners, I'll find the time!"

The week had provided several unforgettable hours. One was a luncheon with Jackie Gleason in the penthouse offices of Gleason Enterprises, Inc. Its walls were bare except for two pictures, Graham reported. One was a tiny photo of TV star, Perry Como. Opposite it, overwhelming in size, was a photo of the mustachioed Gleason in a World War I army uniform. Under it was the title: "Our Founder."

Graham and Gleason talked of spiritual matters. Many columnists had reported the star's solitary patrols around the night-club circuit and his obvious dejection and misery. They said nothing about Graham's visit or any benefit the comedian might have gained. Graham, as usual, said their discussion was confidential.

At the Garden, men scurried about installing seats, erecting the

44

platform, hanging bunting, tying up the loose ends. Overtime crews were furiously chasing gremlins out of new escalators to the upper regions. There would be no time to paint the whitewashed walls. In the basement giant fans were trying vainly to blow away the last fragrant memories of the circus menagerie.

That morning, the *Herald Tribune* had published the first of one hundred front-page boxes with a personal message from the evangelist. His opening statement was:

"On this opening day of the New York Crusade, we are very certain of our expectations. We do not expect to see a city transformed, but we do expect to see individuals transformed. After the crusade is over, New York may appear to be exactly the same —outwardly. But we sincerely believe that thousands of individuals will be very wonderfully changed inwardly in their relationship with God, a change which certainly will make itself felt in better human relationships."

Other papers, equally alert, carried stories by or about the evangelist. Press associations distributed advance "color" stories. At the press office tickets were being issued to journalists from all over the world. Over three hundred required reserved seats for this opening night.

All day Graham's phone rang. There were calls from hundreds of ministers, old friends, and well-wishers, each wanting only five minutes of his time. For eight years he had crusaded across America, saying to new friends, "Whenever you're in a town where I'm preaching, come in and see me."

They came by the hundreds and thousands, but only a few were affronted because Graham's weary secretaries did not immediately throw open his door.

Finally it was the hour for Graham's "quiet time," a period which he observed with Spartan rigor. During it, he exercised his spiritual sinews, prayed, meditated, and worked on his messages. From midafternoon until the hour for the evening service, he saw no one except the waiter who brought his five-o'clock dinner.

Of May 15 he wrote:

"The press today has been remarkable. Almost every paper has front-page stories of the plans and program for tonight.

"After posing some more for the *Life* photographers, I went back to my room for prayer, meditation, study and rest.

"All day long we received hundreds of telegrams from all over

45

the world pledging prayer support. . . . People like Cecil B. De Mille, Roy Rogers and Dale Evans, whole councils of churches, ministerial associations, Baptist associations, even from the little church that I used to be pastor of in Western Springs, Illinois. It seemed that Christians around the world were rallying their prayers on our behalf.

"But all afternoon my heart was in agony. My body was tired and my mind was fatigued. However, the Lord gave me a bit of relaxation and I went to the meeting refreshed in body and spirit with great expectation and believing faith.

"Ruth and I went immediately to the Garden Club where we were met by George Champion, Roger Hull, Erling Olsen and other members of the committee. Here, surrounded by pictures of the famous greats of the fight world, we bowed our heads for the last prayer before we were to go before our first audience in New York. As we went down the steps, we were followed and surrounded by newspaper photographers. Continually I was saying in my heart, 'Oh God, let it be to Thy glory. Let there be no self.'"

6 *But on the day of dedication, gathering his team and thousands of volunteers for prayer and thanksgiving, he donned the mantle of the Lord's "Proclaimer" and confronted the city with its sins ...*

At seven-twenty Billy Graham and committee chairman Roger Hull walked up a short flight of steps that led to their platform seats. It happened so quietly and quickly that only a few people noticed that two chairs which had been empty were suddenly filled.

"I had butterflies in my stomach," Graham would write later that night, "partially due to the fact that I had preached only a few times in the last three months, but also because I always face an audience with a certain amount of fear and trembling. However, to face perhaps the most critical audience of my life gave me complete dependence upon God, and a realization that if anything were to be accomplished this night, He would have to do it."

People had begun to assemble outside the Garden's locked doors in midafternoon. All ages, all shapes, all complexions, they piled out of cars which soon cluttered every parking lot. They spilled out of subways from Brooklyn and the Bronx. They filed out of chartered busses from cities in nearby New England states. Some rode ferries and some rode tubes from Staten Island and Jersey City. Some were salesmen attending conventions, or college girls on vacation, or foreign sailors on shore leave, or missionaries on their sabbatical.

But the big city took little notice of them. The huge garden with its eighteen thousand five hundred seats had been filled so often. At best, compared to the millions who stewed and struggled in the melting pot of Manhattan, it held only a finger pinch of humanity.

Yet, as the currents of people knotted and thickened in the gaudy streets lined with bars and cheap souvenir stores, a wise old police sergeant cocked his eye down the avenue and said, "This looks like a big one. Yessir, like a real big one!"

By five-thirty the sidewalks were packed solid along both sides of the Garden, and groups in the long block between Eighth and Ninth avenues were passing the slow minutes by singing hymns.

At six there was a massive stirring in the streets and the Garden doors opened before thousands of early-comers.

Some came with tickets that promised a seat if they occupied it by seven-fifteen, but thousands merely walked off the street into the gigantic air-cooled auditorium.

Inside, the Garden lobby had never looked like this. A few old-time concessionaires were there, selling soda pop and frankfurters, but the choice spots were occupied by booths that offered Bibles, Gospel recordings, and Billy Graham's books.

A man in a checkered suit threw a dollar on a counter that was recently a bar and said, "Draw one."

"No beer, sir. How about a Coke?"

The man said, "Gimme a pack of Luckies."

"Sorry, sir, we can't sell cigarettes either during the meetings."

The man yelled as if stung by a bee. "The marquee says Billy

Graham's fighting here tonight. What have I got into, a church?"

"That's right, sir. Billy Graham is fighting here, but he's a preacher and not a boxer. Now, how about a nice cold Coke, sir?"

Later a concessionaire complained, "We're starving! You'd think these people would get just a little bit thirsty, but nossir! They rush on in to hear that Graham. That's all they want." Within two weeks he shuttered his place for the duration; but right next door the sale of King James Bibles boomed on.

Along the Garden flanks, dressing rooms had been turned into offices. On the south side, through a shadowy corridor used regularly by pugs, hockey players, and sport fans, one suite was now a seething press room where, at the moment, Mrs. Betty Lowry was trying valiantly to seat three hundred correspondents in the hundred and fifty chairs the Garden had provided.

Further along, an open door revealed a room piled to the ceiling with one hundred thousand crisp, new crusade songbooks.

Circling the corridor across its western end, long tables lay like barricades under signs that said, "Counselor Assignments," "Usher Assignments," and "Choir Information." These were the command posts at which Graham's volunteer battalions would be assigned to their battle stations.

In the north corridor doors led to the team room where members could meet their friends or retire for meditation, a counseling office where strayed or lost sheep could apply for spiritual aid, and the quarters into which Dr. Graham retreated after every service to change his sweat-drenched clothes and hold the hurried, frantic conferences that were to become his way of life.

Whoever entered that vast sanctuary after it was filled with people invariably gasped with amazement. The Garden's main floor, large enough for an ice-hockey rink, was a sea of faces. Starting thirty feet from the pulpit, at the Garden's western end, they ran in blond and brunet ripples to the opposite end, where they tilted upward like a shelving beach.

Circling this sea, rising abruptly over it, in soaring cliffs, were the Garden balconies, peopled now more thickly than any Greenland rookery. Each tier bore a ribbon of patriotic bunting, and up against the ceiling, moving gently in the air-cooled heights, were a dozen unfurled American flags.

"Look!" people would say, pointing. "Look at THAT!"

"That" was the choir, fifteen hundred to two thousand strong every meeting night, all white-shirted and white-bloused, in spectacular array. By seven every night, they were rehearsing. This first night, after only two previous get-togethers, they sat now resting and waiting for their turn.

In the final moments before seven-thirty, one noted that special arrangements had been made for the city's deaf and dumb. In their section a minister stood to translate Graham's message. Another section was reserved for the blind. Another, on the first floor, was for those who came in wheel chairs or on crutches.

Everywhere . . . everywhere! . . . one saw photographers. Probably no news event in the history of Manhattan ever attracted a greater turnout. With the professional effrontery that is their stock in trade, men and women alike stood on tables and balanced on balcony rails in an endless search for "angles."

A *Life* team worked the balcony and main floor, talking to each other with their portable walkie-talkies. Two movie cameras ground away, one on a fixed tower, another on a wheeled platform that skittered about the floor like a giant daddy longlegs.

At the press tables radio reporters with portable tape recorders held their mikes aloft to test acoustics.

Suddenly all eyes were on the platform. Cliff Barrows, song leader extraordinary and platform manager, walked forward to the pulpit. The vast hum of the auditorium subsided. He stood there, boyish and mature at the same time, smiling. To his right, Paul Mickelson manned the console of the giant organ. To his left, Tedd Smith sat behind a tremendous grand piano. Two rows of chairs across the platform held guests, team members, and Dr. Billy Graham.

"Let us praise the Lord in song," Barrows said.

The choir sang "Blessed Assurance" and the audience sang "All Hail the Power of Jesus' Name." Deliberately, Reverend Grady Wilson read Psalm 33:18–22. Dr. Phillips P. Elliott, pastor of the First Presbyterian Church of Brooklyn, led in prayer. And George Beverly Shea sang for the first time, his great solo, "How Great Thou Art."

Roger Hull, committee chairman, welcomed the audience in behalf of the Crusade Committee. Then, like a small boy, he leaned close to the mikes and said, "I'm going to do what I've been asked not to do and I may be soundly spanked for it. But I think you will want to know the most attractive member of the Billy Graham

49

Evangelistic Team . . . Mrs. Billy Graham." He pointed to her sitting modestly in the back row of a box. Smiling, she rose briefly to acknowledge the thunder of sincere respectful applause. Next, he introduced Dr. Billy Graham.

The audience leaned forward, eyes lighting. Graham said things any bright young man would have said. He announced a meeting of ministers. He told a humorous story. He said that this nation had to turn to God or it was doomed. "Amens" fluttered down from balconies as well as the special section that had been reserved for ministers.

When Barrows next took over the podium he laid the crusade policy politely but firmly on the line. This Garden was a sanctuary. This meeting was not entertainment requiring applause. It was an occasion for the worship of God.

"And if somebody says something that makes you feel like shouting for joy," he said, "for the sake of your neighbor, just make it a silent prayer deep in your heart."

That afternoon, a strange thing had happened. Bob Walker of *Christian Life* magazine reported it:

"As Bev Shea, Crusade soloist, described it, 'Throughout the day I had been busy and confident in my expectation of the evening. Late in the afternoon, I found myself suddenly aware of an overwhelming sense of loneliness. Although I had prayed frequently during the day, it seemed as though this might be an attack of Satan against my faith.'

"Shea looked at his watch. It was five o'clock. Meanwhile, Graham in his room had sensed the same need—for the fellowship of his team members in prayer—to believe God for His presence and power in the meeting. First he called Barrows and then Shea. In a matter of moments, the trio had come to Graham's room for a time of prayer that sent them to Madison Square Garden reassured again that the prayers of God's people the world over were behind them. The victory therefore would be His."

Now the evangelist sat quietly, surrounded by an atmosphere of good will. Yet he was not entirely at ease. Trying to describe the moment, he wrote:

"The Garden was filled, insofar as I could see, though I was told there were a couple of hundred seats empty somewhere. What a magnificent sight! I have never seen an audience so well managed, well behaved, reverent and quiet on an opening night.

There was an air of expectancy. I knew before I stepped to the microphone that God was going to work mightily this night.

"Never have we had a choir that sang so beautifully and lustily as this choir. The great Madison Square Garden rang with the voices of fifteen hundred choir members singing 'How Great Thou Art.' Roger Hull made an excellent presentation of the financial situation and needs of the crusade. I was told that something like three hundred members of the press were there, but the platform was high and the photographers were not allowed on it so they did not disturb me. I noticed *Life*, *Look*, *Match*, and saw several newsreel cameras. I knew that the message that I was to give would be carried to the world by the news media. I was silently praying that what I said would glorify God as it went out to the whole world.

"Waiting to ascend the podium, I still did not feel great liberty in my soul and that abandonment that I love to feel when I preach. I looked down and saw Carl Henry, editor of *Christianity Today*, and just as I saw him, he bowed his head in prayer. This seemed representative of thought throughout the world. Suddenly, a great surge of joy swept my soul that brought tears to my eyes. When I stepped to the platform, I knew that God was going to speak through me."

7

Suddenly God's name blazed on every front page and, for the first time in the memory of New Yorkers, religion became a subject about which people on the street were talking . . .

Graham wrote an interesting sentence in his diary on the day after his opening. "Certainly the demons of hell are going to be busy stirring things up in New York," he said. "They are not going to be happy over what has happened."

What had happened over the night of May 15–16 was the

greatest outpouring of praise, approval, and publicity ever given an evangelist by Manhattan's daily press.

Graham was delighted at first and then wary. Was this praise the devil's work, he wondered? His diary reported, "Coverage of the Crusade in the New York press this morning was the largest we have ever had in any city in the world. The New York *Times* devoted nearly three entire pages. They printed my sermon word for word.

"Dr. John Bonnell, pastor of the Fifth Avenue Presbyterian Church, told me today that, in the twenty-three years he has been here in New York City, he has *never* experienced anything like it. Certainly Christ, at least for one day, has been on the front page of every newspaper in New York.

"The New York *Herald Tribune* told of what we were doing and carried several photographs, both on its front page and on some of its other pages. The tabloids, the *Daily News* and *Mirror*, devoted considerable space to the Crusade.

"Then, the evening papers. The *World-Telegram & Sun* came out this afternoon with tremendous coverage, as did the New York *Post.*

"The cartoon in the *Journal-American*, I thought, was priceless. It depicted a boxing ring at Madison Square Garden. In one corner it had the Devil—beaten, dishevelled and discouraged. His handlers, giving him a bottle of whiskey labeled 'Old Nick,' were vigorously trying to resuscitate him. In the other corner, it represented me as a big, strong, muscular prize fighter having won the first round.

"The headline for the column on the front page of the *Journal-American* read: 'Graham Awaits the Devil's Backlash.' While this was amusing and certainly must have gotten a lot of laughs, it was also realistic. There was a great victory last night *and I fully expect Satan to strike from an unexpected quarter.*"

But Satan must have taken to his heels that Thursday in May, lashed by these sinewy headlines and stories:

"The Gospel came to Madison Square Garden last night," proclaimed the New York *Times.* Four of its front-page columns were given to a massive photo of the worshiping crowd. Its reporter said, "It was preached in a simple straight-from-the-shoulder style by the Rev. Dr. Billy Graham—Evangelist Extraordinaire. With the Bible in one hand and the index finger of the other pointing heavenward, Dr. Graham exhorted his listeners to 'Find God—because we can never find ourselves until we find Him.'"

Elsewhere, the *Times* reprinted the text of Dr. Graham's opening sermon verbatim, an honor ordinarily reserved for the remarks of presidents and prime ministers.

Another *Times* story revealed that 112 church delegations were on hand that opening night. Most of them, coming from churches in the metropolitan area, had occupied 6000 of the 19,000 available seats.

Another *Times* article analyzed the crusade's budget of $1,300,000 under this subhead, "But none of money collected here will line the pockets of Graham or his team."

In addition to an extensive news story, the New York *Herald Tribune* published the second of a series of special messages from Billy Graham. In it he emphasized the importance of the Ten Commandments as essential to one's spiritual health:

"A cab driver said the other day, 'You'll never change New York until you cure people of their love of money.' Of course I can't change New York, and I don't propose to, but I will be preaching truths about God that are powerful enough to bring our desires into balance and make us the men we ought to be."

To describe the first meeting, the *Mirror* used this headline, "Billy Battles Devil at Garden." It reported, "Evangelist Billy Graham set out last night on the biggest job of his amazing preaching career—to reform New York. . . . He roared that this city was a Sodom and Gomorrah."

Describing Graham's invitation, it said, "At the end came his appeal to his hearers to come forward to Christ. 'You up there in the balcony,' he said pointing high. 'On the right. On the left. I ask you just one thing. Come down here and join me in a moment of prayer.'

"A hulking man in a brown suit with a yellow tie walked forward from the front row. A gray-haired lady with a flowered hat followed. An Army colonel in summer tan uniform, holding his white-haired wife's hand, came in front of the rostrum. As the spirit spread, more came, four or five hundred altogether."

The New York *News* said, "After 40 minutes of fluid and vibrant eloquence, he folded his arms and bowed his handsome blond head while hundreds in the huge arena trooped forward in answer to his plea to 'give yourselves to Christ.'

53

"By any account, the opening night of Graham's six-week New York crusade—which was three years in preparation—was an unqualified success."

The afternoon papers were even more generous. The New York *Post*, illustrating its story of the opening meeting, used an informal and attractive photograph of Ruth Graham listening to her husband preach.

The *Journal-American* announced, "Graham in Biggest Triumph" and described him as "handsome, golden haired . . . with a voice like an organ and hands that beseech and implore and beckon souls to come to their Maker."

Reporter Madeline Ryttenberg, reporting the moment of invitation, said, "Finally, his voice fell almost to a silky whisper. And the moment had come. For a heart-stopping second it looked as if he hadn't made it. No one moved. There were a few tension-wracked coughs.

"And then a middle-aged man came down the center aisle. He was followed by another, too moved even to wipe the tears from his cheeks. Then by twos and threes, in couples, and in bunches, they came . . . on and on they came, until the space in front of the platform and to each side was jammed."

Dorothy Kilgallen, in an adjacent front-page column, wrote the second in a series of personality articles which she had obtained by visiting Graham in his North Carolina home.

"To Billy Graham," she said, "heaven is a definite place, like Chicago. He can't point it out on the map, but he knows it has pearly gates and streets of gold, and he is headed there as surely as if the one-way ticket were crackling in his pocket."

Bob Considine, one of America's top columnists, commented, "The opening night crowd of 18,500 was remarkable in that this assault on the Satanic citadel of Broadway attracted people who would have been just as much at home at a PTA meeting. The usual Madison Square Garden characters who could use a little reverence were nowhere in sight. The Broadway sharpies were out sharping somewhere. The only untoward note of the evening came while Billy was expounding Isaiah when somebody rolled a photographer for $800 worth of camera equipment."

Andrew Tully, in the *World-Telegram,* after commenting on the usual features, added, "Newsmen who had heard a variety of spellbinders in their day were puzzled by the man in action and

54

his effect on his audience. His sermon was forceful and his preaching technique had verve, but it never approached the spectacular.

"Despite the trappings—the 1500 voice choir, the flowers and bunting—it was the kind of sermon that could have been heard in almost any well-filled church on a Sunday morning. As a Garden attendant in coveralls cracked, 'The guy is under wraps.'

"In a way, that's how it looks. Billy arrived on the platform promptly at the seven-thirty starting time without fanfare. He simply walked up the stairs onto the platform and only the few who happened to be glancing at the right place at the right time saw him . . .

"And when Billy stepped forward to do his job, it was on a low key. He was stern, yet gentle, as he opened with a prayer. 'I want all eyes closed, all heads bowed,' he said. 'Let there be no moving about and no whispering.' Then in the quiet that persisted throughout his sermon, he went to work."

Carol Taylor of the *World-Telegram* said, "Well-tailored in a gray summer suit, white shirt and gray and purple tie, the blond, wavy-haired Billy spoke with the punch, poise and magnetism of a super salesman, rather than the fire of an old-time evangelist.

"He injected notes of humor at frequent intervals and got a laugh when he urged, 'Bring your Bibles and get one with big print. One of the greatest tricks the Devil ever pulled on the American people was printing Bibles in so small a print you couldn't read it, especially those of us who are getting old and have bifocal trouble.'"

Like so many others before her, she gave an accurate eyewitness account of Graham's altar call.

"'I'm going to ask every one of you to get out of your seats and come quietly and stand with bowed heads . . . You need to be born again.'

"The evangelist then folded his arms and stood waiting for the 'inquirers' (Dr. Graham does not call them converts) to file forth to seek counseling.

"As the choir sang . . . the inquirers surged forward as if pulled, to form a semicircle at the foot of the platform. They were young and old . . . an aged, blind Negro man . . . a blonde teen-ager in pale blue party dress. . . .

"'Ladies and gentlemen, this is in answer to the prayers of many people,' said Dr. Graham huskily. 'It's the largest response we've ever had on any opening night anywhere.'"

One of the finest reports of all, and perhaps the most perceptive, was written by Robert Walker, the editor of *Christian Life* magazine. "Graham concluded his message," he reported. "Quietly, he gives the invitation. Those who wish to believe in and receive this Jesus, the Son of God, whom he has presented as the answer to every man's personal problems, are invited to come forward.

"This is the most dramatic moment of the evening. Here is the point on which the prayers of the world have been concentrated. All the preparations will have been in vain if the spirit of God does not convict men and women of their need of the Savior.

"A middle-aged man, then another, starts down the center aisle, then they began to come from all corners of the arena. Men and women. All ages. Some, obviously deeply moved, walked with heads down. Others calmly, purposefully.

"Only the shuffle of feet and the organ are heard. Graham simply stands behind the pulpit. He had given the invitation. Now the Holy Spirit must do the work.

"On and on, they come . . . a young mother tightly clasping a baby, a dignified-looking man with tears unashamedly coursing down his face, a young couple who looked at each other hesitantly before they rose, young boys in sports shirts.

"A famous magazine photographer stands beside us. 'If they don't stop, there won't be anybody left back in the seats,' he says in an awed voice.

"Finally it is over. The organ quiet. Graham directs those who have come forward to the 'inquiry room' where each will meet with a counselor and be given instruction in the life of faith in Christ.

"The Holy Spirit has done its work. The decision cards reveal that 706 have made their decisions for Christ on the first night in tough, sophisticated, irreligious Gotham, the world's most important city."

In all Manhattan only two dissident voices were raised. *One* came from Joseph Lewis, president of the Free Thinkers of America, who issued a manifesto against Billy Graham and his New York Crusade.

The *other* was columnist Murray Kempton of the New York *Post* who uttered this mild dissent: "Billy Graham is a decent honorable man—although a feeble preacher by any proper standards—and he is much too decent to be forced by his commitment to Christ to live even six weeks in a town whose stores hang dirty Christmas cards in their windows in December.

"The faithful who walked down Eighth Avenue from the Garden last night passed, blessedly unseeing, by a store which displays the Holy Bible, some bookkeeper's rewrite of various epistles of St. Paul, and the latest version of Norman Vincent Peale side by side with works geared more to its ordinary clientele like *Are You Over Sex-Ty* and *Sex-ation, 1957.*

"It is not my recollection that the money-changers were peddling Cretan post cards on the side; I think the risen Jesus would have thrown a brick through that store window, and if I have a complaint about Billy Graham, it is that he is too timid . . ."

New York, the center of America's theatrical industry, had to judge Graham's theatricality. *Variety,* the Bible of show business, said that Billy Graham "spells out scripture and verse a la Judy Garland ballads."

Graham's proceedings, it added, were "organized, but not gimmicked the way the cynics would have it. Showmanship is obvious. From the use of lithography, three sheets, twenty-four sheets, and the come-on announcements in the premium rate amusement section of the dailies. So too with the massed chorus and the canyon-deep baritone of George Beverly Shea. But Billy Graham is the star. No doubt about that."

Similarly, the New York *Telegraph* said, under Whitney Bolton's by-line: "He uses music, some lighting effects, some skilled manipulations of the voice and he is proof that Broadway's fanciful layers of odds often enough do not know what they are doing. One of the things they did before he opened at Madison Square Garden with a nut of $900,000 or more and a possibility of collecting unpredictable sums from audiences averaging 18,700 per night was to offer the odds: eight-to-five that Graham would fall on his face in New York. They had few takers—which is well for them. They would have lost miserably . . .

"He is like an excellent salesman: he describes the goods in plain terms, lets you see them and decide on them. He avoids the old, ranting ways and the pulpit thumping. He is a skilled and wise and practised salesman of a commodity he truly believes should be in every home. The shrill ways of the medicine pitch, the arch and subtle ways of the stock and bond pitch, the snarled pitch of the Broadway showman never are heard or seen.

"He is plausibility to the final degree. This is his approach: what he has to give is a plausible thing, an irrefutable thing. It makes great sense. He never for a moment departs from that approach . . ."

No wonder, with press headlines screaming his name, with radio and television presenting him and his assistants . . . no wonder that New York's men and women began to talk about him in a way that no religious personality has been discussed in this generation.

A woman attending a theater along the Rialto a few blocks south found most of the seats empty. She complained to the usher, "It's a pity, but I suppose we will have to get along with half-filled theaters until Billy Graham leaves town."

Tradesmen along the streets leading to Madison Square Garden took their cue and added stocks of Bibles and sacred pictures to their window displays. By the same token, bartenders in the taprooms that had sprung up to accommodate the old sporting crowd found their premises empty. More than one told inquiring reporters, "We are starving to death."

But where was God among all those words? This question filled the minds of team members as they read the endless paragraphs. "I have nourished and brought up children, and they have rebelled against me," Graham had read from Isaiah. "If ye be willing and obedient, ye shall eat the good of the land. But if ye refuse and rebel, ye shall be devoured with the sword, for the mouth of the Lord hath spoken it."

They knew the answer, of course, because it always happened that editors and reporters were interested, first, in a personality and in people. Such things made news, whereas the Gospel message was familiar and threadbare. It might take weeks of Graham's preaching to make them realize that it was not the man but the Word that built revival.

Though New York papers mostly missed the point of the crusade, Graham's audience did not. One who listened was a woman at whose door there began presently one of those amazing events which appear, in themselves, to be trivial, but when added together constitute the essence of revival.

This chain started in Flushing, a section of New York City located on Long Island. One afternoon, a lady who was serving as a counselor in the crusade heard a knock at her door. Answering it, she faced a man who was battered, dirty, and reeking of alcohol.

"I'm trying to get enough money to go home to Lowell, Massachusetts," he said. "I'm sorry to present myself like this, but I have just been robbed."

The lady was frightened, but the man's need was obvious. She said, "I'm afraid money won't help you, but Jesus Christ can. Go out in the back yard. You'll find a chair there. I'll bring you some coffee and something to eat."

As they talked afterward, she realized that his needs were genuine. She and her family were going to the crusade that evening, so she asked him, "Why don't you come along?"

"In this condition? They wouldn't let me in."

"My husband will lend you a clean shirt," she replied.

They arrived at the Garden and found seats. During the sermon, their strange guest seemed to be deeply impressed. When they separated that night he said he might stay in town and go to the Garden again. When Graham issued the invitation at the end of the service the man went forward and accepted Christ.

During his Flushing adventure, the new Christian had become acquainted with four teen-agers. His new experience was so exciting that he had to tell others about it. Next day he invited them to go with him to the Garden. That night all the four teen-agers went forward.

Those four, in turn, began to spread God's message to others. Then they all got together, rented a bus, and attended the meeting as a unit. Almost fifty of them went forward.

Today, these youngsters are working with the Baptist Church in the Corona area. Throughout the crusade they continued to lengthen and strengthen the chain that had started with what seemed to be an impossibly weak link—a man, beaten, robbed, exhausted, knocking at the door of a Christian home.

8

The Big Town shook its head in wonder, then went about its business, but a thoughtful few began to ponder what attraction led those thousands to the Garden . . .

No doubt about it, the Big Town was confounded. That outpouring of publicity in behalf of a minister of the Gospel both startled and baffled its historians. Typically, they shrugged it off.

"His show will be a cold turkey in two weeks," a Broadway pundit avowed.

"His voice is already gone," a horse player said. "He won't last that long. I'll lay odds on it."

Yet many more thoughtful citizens began to be deeply concerned about what was going on at Madison Square Garden.

Graham preached each night with reckless disregard of the voice that sounded at times like a rusty saw but healed after a few days into an instrument as scathing as a scourge or as caressing as a breeze.

He knew better than anyone that this was the time when thousands would begin to appraise his ministry. As the Garden filled each night, as inquirers came forward by the hundreds, and as word-of-mouth comment spread, people would ask questions of each other and of those who had been to a service. . . .

What persuaded so many thousands to buck heat and traffic to fill those Garden seats?

What led so many men, women, and young people to respond to Graham's invitation?

What? What? What?

In the beginning, only one man began to surmise the whole answer: Dr. Billy Graham, whose diary for May 16 said:

"In the afternoon I prepared my message for tonight entitled 'Sin.' I prayed a great deal during the afternoon and slept for about an hour. I rarely am able to sleep in the afternoon and this was one of those rare times. My throat has grown increasingly sore. I am looking to the Lord for victory tonight.

"Grady and I arrived at Madison Square Garden. A group of the men who were to sit on the platform were gathered . . . and we had prayer together. How wonderful to see Jack Wyrtzen. Jack has stood with us all through the preparation period of this crusade. His fellowship in this ministry has been of the greatest possible encouragement to me.

"We went to the platform and again we could sense the power and presence of God. Between thirteen and fourteen thousand people had gathered, which I believe sets a record in our crusades for the second night, with perhaps the exception of Glasgow.

"My throat being so sore, I did not feel liberty in preaching, but I did feel power. There is a vast distinction between liberty and power. Sometimes when I have felt the least liberty in preaching, I have sensed the greatest spiritual power. I could tell that the Lord was hammering home His message to the people. When the invitation was given, they came more quickly than they did last night, and 545 people streamed down the aisles and from the balconies . . ."

Three days later:

"What days these are! Never in my ministry have I sensed the presence of God in any place as I have at Madison Square Garden. Friday night I think I preached with greater liberty and power than at any other time in my life. I do not ever remember having had such complete abandonment and freedom of the Spirit. It seemed that the whole Garden had been supercharged with the power of the Holy Spirit. When the invitation was given 785 people came in response.

"Friday night I preached on the Person of Christ. I emphasized his virgin birth, his glorious atonement and his victorious resurrection. The Lord honored it and brought many to the Savior. That night I came home feeling that a great burden had been lifted. I felt that we were gradually getting over the hump. . . ."

His entry for Saturday:

"Saturday night Madison Square Garden was filled, and I think the number responding to the invitation was even greater than Friday, though I have not received any official count.

"I am trying to commit to memory one portion of Scripture each day, though I am afraid this is almost too much and I am not retaining them as I should.

"My passage for Saturday was especially significant: II Chronicles 20:15—'Thus saith the Lord unto you, Be not afraid nor dismayed by reason of this great multitude; for the battle is not yours, but God's.' All day long that passage rang in my ears. However, before the service Saturday I seemed to sense that Satan was putting up a mighty battle. I almost expected that there would be a scream in the audience, as I have sometimes seen; that would be what I consider demonic possession. I even expected to hear a shot fired, or some outburst from the enemy. I went over to Madison Square Garden in great agony of the heart, realizing that I was having a spiritual battle.

"Preaching was not easy. I preached on Paul's sermon at Mars Hill . . . but there was not the liberty or power that I felt the night before. However, when the invitation was given, I think even more came. There seems to be no let-up in the stream of humanity coming to Christ. I have made the invitation hard and difficult, and yet as clear as I believe it can possibly be made. Yet, they come!"

Yet they come!

Each night, each week, each month! Coming forward down the Garden aisles, proving that something mystical and wonderful was happening. But most local folk, having lived on superficialities for so long, could imagine only that another superficiality was the cause of it all.

At first they credited Graham's personality. "There he is," wrote Phyllis Battelle of INS, "backed by the 1,500 voice choir that swells its melodic timbre to match the power of this tall, straight man with probing eyes who looks so alone, and yet so strong. Hundreds of spotlights converge attentively on the taut frame in the tan suit, and the hush is so dramatic you can hear your conscience screaming aloud."

Stanley Rowland, Jr., wrote in the *Times,* "Mr. Graham loosens his tie and speaks with clear urgency. He is a tall, commanding figure (six feet, two inches) and conviction seems to vibrate through his intense body. In firm, sweeping gestures, his arm goes straight out with a finger pointing, then up with the fist clenched, then down in a short arc to the Bible on the podium as he drives

62

a point home with a Biblical quotation. Sweat begins to glisten on his face."

They saw only an orator, effective, dynamic.

Others saw a "regular guy." In Washington last year, when he was to speak before the National Press Club, there was much discussion that their bar should be closed during his visit. He confounded the committee by visiting the bar and drinking an orange juice.

He was a golfer but not a good one, and the public learned of it from newspaper stories that quoted his chagrined remark, "The Lord answers my prayers everywhere but on the golf course."

He was modest: "Every time I see my name up in lights, it makes me sick at heart, for God said He will share His glory with no man. Pat me on the back and you will ruin my ministry. If God should take his hands off my life, my lips would turn to clay. I'm no great intellectual, and there are thousands of men who are better preachers. You can't explain me if you leave out the supernatural. I am but a tool of God."

He was God-driven, too. Many New York preachers spoke as if their Sunday sermons were an added chore for which they had scant time or taste. Graham said, "I am an evangelist because I cannot help it. If I restrained myself, I would burst from sheer pressure."

Members of the Broadway mob that stood watching the nightly torrent of humanity pouring into the Garden admitted his remarkable qualities but felt that they were not, of themselves, enough to attract an attendance of 575,000 in the first month. Or to persuade 18,500 inquirers to seek spiritual assistance.

They argued in favor of his showmanship. Broadway, that neon-lighted galaxy of Pulitzer-prize dramas, pizza palaces, and flea circuses, was the home of showmanship. So its experts slipped into the Garden to watch and learn.

They discovered a church!

Its choir was bigger than any other church, its loud-speaker more powerful, its soloists more talented (Bev Shea, Ethel Waters, Jerome Hines), its auditorium was larger (19,200 including standees), its pulpit was higher, and its height could be adjusted electrically by pressing a button.

But they discovered another thing. The Bible! Graham held it open in his hand, raised it over his head, slashed the air with it!

It made a white blur, a stabbing sword point, a blazing beacon. Even those in the far reaches of the balcony could see its gleaming face.

Each night Graham told his audience, "Bring your Bibles! Let's see how many have brought their Bibles. Hold them over your heads. Hold them so we can count them!"

As the weeks passed, the upthrust arms in his audience multiplied until they waved as thickly and beautifully as ripe Kansas wheat. Red Bibles, and white, and black, and tan! Bibles by the thousands that rested presently on laps in subways, and trains, where other thousands saw them; or opened before prying eyes in a Broadway bus, or lay on a table while one friend told another of the joy of finding God in the Garden.

A young woman wrote Dr. Graham, "As you suggested, I began to carry my Bible to and from work. At first, I was shy about being seen with it, but when I saw people unashamedly reading scandal magazines and sex novels, I said, 'What have I got to be afraid of? It's God's Word. It's His message to all!' So I brought it out of my purse and held it up, sometimes even when I was hanging onto a subway strap, and it was wonderful to see how many people edged over to look and then to sneak a few minutes of Bible reading over my shoulder."

Was that showmanship? Not the Broadway brand, certainly.

Well, the crusade's success had to be due to *something*. Big names? Star names? Maybe that was it? Personalities did attend, many, many celebrities . . .

Jane Pickens, the singer . . . Ed Sullivan of TV . . . Vice-President Nixon . . . socialite Mrs. C. V. Whitney . . . screen star Sonja Henie . . . actress Gene Tierney . . . Alvin Dark, Carl Erskine, and a benchful of ballplayers . . . Greer Garson . . . Perle Mesta . . . Adolph Zukor . . . Pearl Bailey . . . Jack Dempsey . . . Dale Evans spoke from the pulpit . . . so did Stuart Hamblen, song writer . . . and even Chief Tarari, a reformed and born-again head-hunter from the wilds of Peru, wearing feathers, beads, and a brotherly smile.

No, there was surely another answer. How about those puffs in the columns? How about publicity?

Walter Winchell said, "Billy Graham's crusade to save New York from sin apparently has clicked. Midtown bookstores report the biggest demand for the Bible in years."

Dorothy Kilgallen said, "Bowery derelicts are making a point of drifting up to the Madison Square Garden area hoping for and getting handouts from kindly visitors in the Billy Graham meetings."

Hadn't Graham defended his publicity methods in public?

"I am aware that some ministers are not in complete accord with our methods of evangelism. Some people object to publicizing religion. But every organization that has anything worth while to offer the public seizes the opportunity provided by the miracle of modern communications. We are presenting the greatest product in the world. So why not give it at least as much promotion as a bar of soap?"

Graham's mother walked to the pulpit one night and told 19,200 people about the first verse of Scripture she had taught Billy. "It was from Proverbs 3:6. 'In all thy ways acknowledge Him and He shall direct thy paths.' No mother could be more proud of her son's living up to that rule of life than I am," she said.

A stunt, a gimmick, a publicity weinie, the smart boys said, "Like Liberace and his mother."

"And what about all the help he gets from *Life* magazine? Sure it's publicity. How about that July 1 issue with Billy on the cover and all those pages inside?"

A newsstand operator near the Garden who sold out immediately said, "Sure I read the piece and I'm still wonderin' what it's about. 'Dedicated deciders,' *Life* called 'em. I saw them pictures and they looked more like oddballs to me, guys with a fix of some sort who'd got into the Garden and unloaded their troubles."

He was nearer right than any of the others.

John Goldner, the coldly hard-boiled manager of Madison Square Garden, said, "It's been an amazing thing. I still don't understand how he keeps them coming."

Andrew Tully, of the *World-Telegram,* had a pat answer:

"What New Yorkers have seen during this smooth-running crusade is the latest model in the successful American male. Billy Graham is part Dick Nixon and part Jack Kennedy, with overtones of the young executive behind a Madison Avenue desk. He is the completely modern man who eagerly uses every modern gadget to sell his merchandise.

"Around him he has gathered a staff that is a curious mixture

65

of prairie town corn, Rotary Club exuberance and the hard-boiled approach of a political campaign headquarters.

"While master of ceremonies Cliff Barrows exudes his folksy unctuousness on the stage, a sharp-minded public relations staff checks figures and TV ratings, and turns out the mimeographed literature that keeps Billy Graham in the public eye. Like Vice-President Nixon, Billy has accepted the press as a potential ally. He is amiably accessible to individual reporters, and they have discovered he will answer questions with a minimum of artful dodging. He has the business-like directness Mr. Nixon employs so well, and the kind of wholesome candor and clean-cut manner reminiscent of your Senator Kennedy. He is a man it is difficult to dislike, even if you disapprove his tactics, because he is so effortlessly agreeable."

One and all, according to Graham and his team, missed the main point. In complicated, involuted, egocentric, double-talking Manhattan, Graham's secret was too simple. A leader of the Christian Businessman's Committee of Brooklyn told a newsman, "It's simply the miracle of people being born again. Not one or a dozen or a hundred. But thousands!"

The Big Town's wags began to jest irreverently. They called Graham's crusade a "Christ-orama." Smart alecks asked in mock seriousness, "Are you a born-againer?"

What they were talking about, they had no idea. But those who went forward in the Garden knew. Their experiences were reported usually at team meetings. Many of these people who made decisions wrote long, glowing letters. Letters of thanks! Letters of gratitude! Any outsider reading them would shake his head and say, "Incredible! Incomprehensible!" The team understood. Graham understood. But not New York, not yet.

Newsmen searched hundreds of documents, asking themselves, "Why are these people so happy?" The letters told them clearly enough:

From a woman of Rego Park . . . "I don't know how we got along during our four years of married life without the Lord as head of our home. Words cannot describe the transformation that has come over us. A poor description would be to say that it felt like a gust of good, clean, country air swept into me and has not left—or never will, I am sure."

66

From a girl in New Jersey . . . "I want to write to tell you how wonderful my life has been in the last few weeks. I find wonderful peace and satisfaction, something I never experienced before. I am also reading the Book of John which contains so many truthful and meaningful messages. I find, also, that I never feel alone anymore, no matter what I am doing. I feel that Christ is with me in every move I make and it is a glorious feeling."

From a man in Westport, Connecticut . . . "Dear Billy Graham, I sat up there in the second balcony quite sure that salvation was not for me even though I am and have been a very active church member. But I began praying that *others* might be moved to receive Him and to come forward. It was then that the miracle happened. It seemed that God practically yanked me out of my seat. I tried to tell Him and myself that this was all nonsense and the reason I was hurrying along was to get out of the Garden. But, no! I found myself standing with hundreds of others at the pulpit, really at the foot of the Cross.

"The next day . . . some friends . . . we went out and celebrated and I got drunk, and my new world fell apart. I prayed but the Spirit was gone. Then I came back to the Garden one noon in the hope of speaking to an associate evangelist. I finally found one and he was wonderfully kind. There were no empty rooms so we sat in the huge auditorium all by ourselves. By means of Scriptures, he assured me of God's forgiveness. I wept and felt embarrassed. His prayer was beautiful and reassuring. So my heartfelt thanks go out to you and to those wonderful people associated with the crusade who have brought Christ very close to thousands *and even to me.*"

Report from a worker . . . "I was handing out passes on a street corner when I ran into a seedy-looking character that I invited to the Garden. He said, 'If I had a cup of coffee, I might be interested.' He was shabby, unshaven with a long beard, and had a whiskey bottle in his hip pocket. I finally got him into a balcony seat. During the service, he began to cry when the choir sang 'How Great Thou Art.' Through the sermon, he sobbed quietly. When Dr. Graham gave the invitation, he leaped to his feet and led all the others down the aisle. That night he threw away his bottle, promised to save his money and buy a Bible and said his craving for alcohol had vanished forever."

Report from a counselor . . . "This is about a young business woman, successful, about thirty, who had been unable to find peace. She had paid a psychiatrist $500 for four consultations without receiving any benefit. She felt that she ought to give up her job. One Saturday, she tuned to the Garden broadcast. It seemed to her that Graham was talking directly to her alone. As she listened, she became aware that her anxieties were quieting. Could it be, she wondered, that Jesus was the answer? Kneeling beside her TV set, she prayed.

"'When I rose, it was unbelievable,' she reported. 'I was exhilaratingly happy. Energy suffused me. I cleaned the living room and did the washing. This sounds crazy but it was midnight when I hung the last of it on the line. Next day, I went to church for the first time in years and it was wonderful. Suddenly, I remembered my next date with the psychiatrist.'

"Wondering what to do, she hurried to the counseling room at the Garden. There, she was given guidance from the Bible. She left, a strong, self-confident girl.

"But that is not the end," the counselor reported. "She next formed a team of fifteen other people that she met at the Garden and they became tireless in telling others of what Christ had done for them. One day, when it seemed that the crusade might end in July, she delivered a petition to Dr. Graham that she and her team had obtained. It begged him to stay on and promised unlimited support. It was signed by 532 people."

Report from a counselor . . . "I met a man tonight who seemed deeply moved. He told me, 'I've been here several times but tonight I had to come forward.' I asked him if he had any previous religious experience. He said, 'Indeed I have. I accepted Christ when I was a young man. I'm a church member in a Fifth Avenue church. But tonight, my conscience drove me forward.'

"This inquirer is a doctor of languages and a professor in one of the city's largest colleges. He is an answer, I think, to those who say that Dr. Graham's preaching cannot move an 'intellectual.'"

Report from a counselor . . . "This is to report on a call I received from a young man from Iran who came forward recently. He had completed his medical training and set up a successful practice in Los Angeles. He came to the Garden while considering the offer of a fine research job here. He and his wife both came

Graham's powerful preaching drew crowds to Madison Square Garden night after night. In the city where shows and sporting events traditionally started at 8:30 p.m. or later, the team was warned against the earlier starting time. But New Yorkers converged on the Garden in record-breaking numbers.

The service in Yankee Stadium on July 21 provided this spectacular aerial photograph. The famous baseball stadium had never seen such a crowd. At midafternoon its manager predicted a crowd of 50,000. "New Yorkers won't come out for religion," he said. By seven o'clock 100,000 from metropolitan New York jammed every available foot of standing room in the outfield and 20,000 others had been turned away. The choir of 4,000 voices filled an entire section from third base to home plate. Other stadium crowds: 81,841 saw the Yankees play the Boston Red Sox in 1938. Jehovah's Witnesses numbering 84,000 gathered in 1953. Graham's 100,000 plus 20,000 turned away broke every record.

Part of Graham's mission was to reach the unchurched. In addition to preaching several messages in outdoor venues, he visited one-on-one with people, such as this resident in one of the poorer sections of New York City.

forward. He tells me he has now decided to become a medical missionary and to return to his homeland to do what he can to help the people of his own nationality."

Report from a counselor . . . "This young woman of twenty-nine has been married for four years to a young man in the Army. She has felt an increasing need for God. Raised in a Roman Catholic convent in Indo-China where her father was a government official, she studied and considered many religions and finally settled on Yoga, which she was studying when curiosity brought her to the Garden. On her first visit she went forward to accept Christ. Returning home, she told her husband of what had happened and they came together the next night and he, too, gave his life to Jesus. As soon as possible, when he is released from the Army, they hope to return to Indo-China as Christian missionaries."

Report from an adviser . . . "I met this businessman from Wheeling, West Virginia, one afternoon when he walked into the lobby and went from person to person, asking for someone to help him. He had been to a service during an earlier insurance convention, and had even gone forward, but the whole idea of salvation was too much for him to understand, so he left hurriedly to catch his train.

"At the station, some folks who had also attended the meeting glimpsed the green envelope handed him in the counseling room. They began to chat together and to testify what God had done in their lives.

"The man said he had those people in his mind all the way home. They seemed so contented and happy. In Wheeling he told his wife and three children what he had done. As he spoke, he decided he had to return to the Garden. He drove the distance in one day.

"We talked that afternoon, he attended the evening service, and we talked again later. This time he acknowledged his sins and received Christ into his heart. Later I had dinner with him and he could hardly contain himself. His one ambition was to hurry back to his employees and family so he could testify to what had happened, and hold Bible studies and prayer meetings with them."

Letters, post cards, reports, jottings, scribblings, in a dozen lan-

69

guages, reflected New York's spiritual hunger. Day after day the evidence accumulated. One night Billy Graham summed it up for himself in these words from his diary:

"Oh, the spiritual hunger of New York! The question that burns itself in my soul is: what have the preachers been preaching? If they could only realize that these people are hungry for a simple Gospel message and an opportunity to receive Christ. One precious old man grabbed my hand and said, 'Mr. Graham, I found Christ last night. What a difference!' And then he broke into tears. How many stories we are now hearing about people whose lives are changed. A show girl on Broadway who had come from Texas three years ago had succumbed to narcotics, alcohol, and sex—yet she has been gloriously converted."

9

They asked, what's he got, this Billy the Kid? Well, he had a team gathered from three continents, larger, more versatile, more dedicated than ever . . .

Let the cynics mouth their impious jests.

Let disgruntled, nose-out-of-joint malcontents speak disaster from their puny pulpits.

Let the giants and the pygmies, the sincere and the short-sighted, the unbiased and the bigots expound their rubrics.

Let the sprawling city lie brooding, undecided, baffled, perplexed, at the enigma in the Garden.

In one conference room in the Hotel New Yorker each Saturday morning, there was an oasis of conviction; an upper room, by the way, where dedicated men and women gathered in behalf of a mission and a Gospel they believed to be indisputable, incontestable, irrefutable, and unimpeachable.

This was the weekly meeting of the Billy Graham team. While others debated, they were already locked in battle with the devil on a dozen fronts. They were the "old pros" of evangelism, feeling their way through Manhattan midnight gloom with the light that shines from Genesis to Revelation.

An attractive-looking group, the men were mostly lean and supple. The women were well-groomed, buoyant, and charming. Many were ordained ministers, others were lay men and women. All were filled with that inner light that confounded so many New Yorkers.

This meeting was a time for fellowship and for proclaiming the newborn. The Reverend Howard Jones, temporary team member borrowed from a Cleveland pastorate, faced his fellows and this is the story he told:

"A prosperous-looking man of about forty came to me at the Garden. 'I'm here as a last resort,' he said. 'My problem is crushing me. If I can't solve it, I'll kill myself.' His eyes were sleepless and sunken.

"He was a man who had everything; charming wife, two lovely children, fine home, a good business. But his heart was eaten with hatred. He hated his father as an animal hates his foe. You could see the hate dripping from his lips when he spoke of his boyhood, of the event that shattered his love for the father he worshiped. All the years since had fed his hate till it flamed higher and higher.

" 'I know it's consuming me,' he said. 'What can I do?'

"We went to the Bible. I showed him that God is a loving God and a forgiving God. 'But I've hated too long to stop,' he cried. 'I can't stop! I can't stop!'

"I told him, 'If you put things right with your father, and if you go to God through Jesus Christ, he will help you.' 'I don't believe it,' he said. 'But I want to think it over.'

"Next day, he phoned me and his voice rang with triumph. 'I've talked to my father,' he said. 'I told him my hate is gone. I told him I was sorry for my thoughts and actions. I didn't think I could ever say such words but I did, and I feel good.'

"The other night, this gentleman came forward in the Garden. What a difference! He stood straight and his eyes were clear. It was my privilege to be with him when he accepted Christ as his Savior."

At some team meetings, they heard the reading of letters written to Graham, his associates, or workers they had met at the Garden. One morning they heard this:

"Dear Brother Billy . . .

"I write this note to relate an incident that took place recently on a subway train and in our Prayer Room at the Garden. After you had preached on the subject of Hell and Judgment, an old man and two teen-age boys left the Garden and got on a subway train. They were not together. . . .

"The old man was standing up in the car, leaning his bowed head down into the crook of one arm as he wept aloud and cried out in anguish so everyone could hear him, beating his clenched fist on the wall as he wept, and shouted, 'Oh, why didn't I go forward tonight? Why, oh, why? Why didn't I do it tonight?'

"The boys said that no one sought to help the old man, but that their own hearts were painfully smitten because of the fact that they had not accepted Christ that night either. On the very next night, those two boys sought me out in the Prayer Room at about six o'clock tearfully and tremblingly, to ask me if I would help them to accept Christ as their Savior and Lord right then and there. They did not dare to wait for the service lest the Holy Spirit be grieved away from them, even as the poor old man feared that he had done.

"Well, giving God the glory, and that's for sure, it was my happy privilege to lead the boys to Christ for salvation full and free.

"Yours in prayer . . ."

After the reading, all the eyes around that table were warm and some were wet. This was the stuff that replenished the blood and revived weary spirits. These brisk young men and women had come from three continents. Most of them had left comfortable homes to enlist "for the duration" in the New York Crusade, and were drawing on their savings in order to stay, because no man can live at a good hotel in New York, eat in its restaurants, and pay for laundry, cleaning, transportation, and phone calls on the fifteen dollars per day allocated by the crusade budget. Yet there was no discontent, no regret. They were an amazing group.

On May 16, 1957, Graham wrote . . .

"I turned the inquiry room over to Joe Blinco entirely tonight and went directly to my room because I was very wet from perspiration, felt I was catching cold, and my throat was unbearably sore. I hope these precious ones who came forward will understand. I long ago discovered that I cannot do all the Lord's work. That's the reason we have a team.

"My major responsibility is preaching the main message, and I have entrusted many facets of the other work to other team members. I have felt that many evangelists wore themselves completely out by trying to do everything themselves. Blessed is the man who can surround himself with capable, dedicated, spiritual specialists; and then entrust them with responsibility and commit their work to God."

The following week he wrote, "We had a team social today. Lee Fisher did a magnificent job of getting various team members to sing. My, how much musical talent we have on the team! I didn't realize it. They were great. We sang some old love songs and then ended with Gospel choruses and hymns, then a devotional period. Everyone relaxed.

"The team seems to be more united now than I can ever remember. Certainly, the Lord has meshed our hearts together for this crusade. I think these socials are a necessity in order to let the team relax, let off steam, and let their hair down. What a wonderful dedicated, thrilling group they are! How loyal and surrendered to Christ! I am proud of every one of them."

Graham sees God's hand in the selection of each team member. Grady Wilson has been his companion since high-school days. He is the only one that Graham chides publicly, pointing to his solid silhouette and admonishing him to eat less fried chicken. "We were boys together," he tells his audience. "Grady always was a handful to handle so his mother kept a razorstrop hanging in the kitchen. Over it she hung a sign that said, 'I Need Thee Every Hour.'"

Beverly Shea, former insurance clerk, radio announcer, and student at Chicago's famous Moody Bible Institute, came to Graham as a singer on the radio program which his tiny church sponsored in Western Springs, Illinois.

He met Cliff Barrows in Asheville, North Carolina, at a Youth for Christ rally. Barrows, hardly out of his teens, had stepped forward to substitute for a missing song leader, and a dedicated partnership began.

Willis Haymaker, probably the most experienced all-round revival executive in America, was a banker until he felt called to work in the evangelistic field. A long-time friend of Graham's father, he had retired from a successful career of helping such celebrated crusaders as Gypsy Smith of Great Britain, when young Billy, the son of his old friend, began to attract national attention. So Haymaker returned to the wars to become crusade director. This year, his daughter, Martha, took leave from her job as a schoolteacher to organize the crusade's hospitality department, and became the team's first second-generation member.

Graham found Jerry Beavan editing a Bible-study magazine and teaching at Northwestern Schools, borrowed him to "look after the press" during his 1950 crusade through New England, and has depended on him ever since for the delicate task of preparing an indifferent city for a forthcoming crusade. Beavan, who began his labors, both in London and New York, two years ahead of the first crusade service, is Graham's executive secretary and public-relations adviser.

Whatever the criticism, Graham feels that he is on solid ground. His great drive is to reach the unchurched, the men, women, and young people who normally never attend any place of worship. To reach them, he has adopted and modernized a technique as old as Christianity.

Some evangelists are fond of saying that Jesus Christ was the first to use a team when he summoned his Apostles. Later, the Apostle Paul was said to have sent a personal representative to the churches of Asia Minor two years before his own evangelizing visit.

Among nineteenth-century evangelists, D. L. Moody, a great organizing genius, employed a corps of assistants to recruit thousands of church workers into troops of ushers, choristers, doormen, personal workers, prayer leaders, and flying squadrons of doorbell ringers.

When Billy Sunday invaded New York in 1917 in his "Christ for New York" campaign, he was assisted by Homer Rodeheaver as choir leader, his son as business manager, and so many other assistants that the revival committee had to provide a huge private residence to house them. His crusade publicity was supervised by a genius named Ivy Lee, who was also public relations adviser of John D. Rockefeller, Sr.

To reach the unchurched, Graham first took his ministry to theaters and auditoriums. Following precedent, he preached next in specially built tabernacles of wood or canvas. When crowds out-

74

grew even those roomy structures he moved to football stadiums and boxing arenas.

With each step, he won more listeners, but he also increased the complexity of managing his crowds and the churches that supported each crusade.

He has never claimed that he invented the team plan, although his success in using it makes him its outstanding protagonist. His needs, as they developed, were the force that formed the formula.

Nevertheless, as a result of global experience, the concept has crystallized around eleven primary members. Wilson, Barrows, Shea, Beavan, and Haymaker are the hard core. Others are:

Tedd Smith, pianist; Paul Mickleson, organist, who has now joined RCA Victor; Reverend Leighton Ford, associate evangelist; Reverend Joe Blinco, England's leading Methodist evangelist; Mrs. Betty Lowry, press; Charles Riggs, counseling trainer.

New York presented knotty problems not found in other cities. In the beginning, many Protestant groups were so discouraged and lonely amid the city's vast non-Protestant population that they could not imagine any campaign that would succeed. Their rejuvenation became a crusade objective.

Because so many churches were weak, the manpower usually available for volunteer work in a community did not exist. In consequence, the regular staff was augmented by part-time employees who were veterans of other crusades.

Originally the crusade budget provided for the living and travel expenses of twenty-two team members. All their salaries, as well as Graham's, were paid in full by the Billy Graham Evangelistic Association of Minneapolis, the non-profit enterprise which handles Graham's "Hour of Decision" broadcasts. Fourteen more were budgeted for periods of one to six weeks. These specialists were to be paid travel and living costs plus modest honorariums.

However, by the end of the crusade, no less than sixty-five dedicated young Christians had served either part or full time.

One group member was Patricia Campion, former follower of Great Britain's Young Communist League, who was converted during the London Crusade. Subsequently, entering full-time Christian activity, she came to New York to work among various social groups.

Another was the Reverend Tom Allen, brought from Scotland especially to conduct the Ministers' Workshops. A leader in the field of parish evangelism, he possessed both specialized knowledge and a knack for imparting it that was available in no other person.

A successful business executive once asked a Graham aid, "How's your outfit set up? What's your table of organization? Who reports to whom?"

"Nobody reports to anyone, sir," the aid replied.

"How in thunder do you know what to do next?"

"We do whatever needs to be done."

The businessman shook his head, baffled, "But who does what? Don't you have job descriptions?"

"Oh, those!" the aid said brightly. "We certainly do, sir. We had every job written up for the benefit of the New York committee, but each week something new came up. Inside a month, our duties were all scrambled around again."

Actually Graham makes final all important policy decisions, settling most of them prior to the opening night. For counsel he leans heavily on the experience and prayers of his oldest associates. In day-to-day operations each man knows what to do to complete his segment of the pattern that must provide the crowds of unchurched that Graham must reach. If a man needs help, he appeals to another team member but rarely to Graham.

Beavan once described the program as "a one-man show" during the months while things are being organized, and then a few weeks before the opening, other members arrive and take over their jobs—like Lorne Sanny, who has charge of counselor training. Past experience told him he would need about five thousand trained counselors for the crowds expected. He knew it would take seven meetings to train them. So he planned accordingly. After all his volunteers were trained, he packed up and went on to other projects.

Once a team member has been assigned to an area of work or given a project, he is pretty much on his own. This lack of supervision has caused flutterings in the stomachs of big business executives who know what happens among their own juniors when they are left without directives or at least the threat of the boss's big whip. As crusade events run their course, these faint hearts are usually reassured.

A team member faces two other stringent responsibilities.

First, he must be ready to preach, pray, debate, or lecture before community groups at the drop of a hint.

Second, he must be ready to offer counsel to the needy at any hour around the clock.

A typical day during the New York Crusade saw associate evangelist Grady Wilson making a radio talk; Mel Dibble, who produced the TV program called "Impact," addressing a group at the Metropolitan Life Insurance Company; Reverend Leighton Ford conducting a Bible class for new converts; Reverend Abdul Haqq leading a pre-service prayer meeting; Reverend Howard Jones preaching at the Faith Baptist Church in west New York.

On one Sunday the Reverend Joe Blinco preached at 8:15 in the Bronx and at 11 A.M. in Newark, N. J. Howard Butt, Texas lay evangelist, preached on Long Island in the morning, in up-state New York in the afternoon, and in Manhattan that evening. Dr. Paul Rees was at Grace Episcopal Church in New York. Dr. Ralph Mitchell was at Union Evangelist Church in Corona, Long Island. Mel Dibble was at the First Baptist in Patchogue, Long Island. Lane Adams was in Brooklyn for an eleven o'clock service and at Moulton Memorial in Newburgh, New York, that afternoon. Mrs. Lila Trotman had speaking assignments and so did a half-dozen others.

Add to full-time duties a nightly Garden meeting, private conferences with converts whose backbones need stiffening, trips to suburban communities by day and night, and it is easy to understand why most team members lost weight.

No wonder Graham was proud of them. No wonder a diary entry said, "I think these socials are a necessity to let the team relax."

His own contribution at each Saturday-morning meeting was surprising to some of his committee associates. They expected him to play the Big Boss, laying out the next week's plan of action. Then one of them, a banker, asked a young team member what went on behind those closed doors.

"What's the pitch? How does Graham keep you fellows on the ball?"

The young aid looked slightly startled and said, "Dr. Graham tells us things like we ought to be more kind to people and more unselfish. He reminds us that folks in New York are watching us. And that we should be equally courteous to everyone from bellboys and maids in the hotel up to the big people who are helping with the crusade."

The man exploded. "Is that all?"

"Oh no. We pray. Then we talk about the people we've met. And we tell about helping someone to find Jesus. Some of the stories almost tear your heart out."

The team that Graham organized for the New York Crusade was the largest, most versatile, most dedicated of his career. Each man knew why he was a member, and needed no reminder. This was the battle that the Christian world watched.

Each man knew what he had to do!

10 *While New York pondered, already the team lay locked in battle. To each, this crusade was the Big One, the fight to be fought to a finish . . .*

The Graham team is composed of razor-sharp specialists in an exacting profession. One must be a strategist but not a schemer, humble but not servile, resolute but not obstinate, persuasive but not pedantic. This is a singular combination of personal qualities. Additional standard equipment is a cast-iron stomach, nerves of steel, and a heart of gold.

Willis G. Haymaker, old friend of the Graham family, possesses every attribute mentioned. To him went the pre-crusade assignment of organizing global prayer.

It is almost impossible to overstate Graham's faith in the power of prayer. Examine his former crusades and you find his call to prayer ringing out each time.

"I hope New York City will become the most prayed-for spot on the face of the earth."

Making that hope come true became Willis Haymaker's first task.

Like any good executive, he set a goal. The global goal was two hundred and fifty thousand prayer partners in one hundred countries.

The New York goal was a prayer group in every city block.

The methodology of success is not a subject for this chapter. It is enough to know that Mr. Haymaker knew precisely what to do: how to find and enlist many willing collaborators including global, national, and local prayer organizations; how to work with volunteers who would give their time without stint. What a pity that so many did so much that space is not at hand to hail their works.

Having made needed arrangements, Haymaker dispatched letters to key people in key situations. All previous crusade cities retained the nucleus of Graham's old prayer organization. Letters went to each former chairman, saying:

"The New York Crusade presents every praying Christian with the greatest challenge of the century . . .

"If we did not believe that individuals across America and around the world would be praying for us, we would not dare attempt this crusade . . .

"We are asking you, as our crusade prayer chairman, to reactivate your cottage prayer groups and join with others in united prayer for revival in New York.

"The day of the beginning of this program is Tuesday, April 1, 1957."

The response was amazing.

To supervise New York recruiting, the Crusade Executive Committee directed the appointment, from among prominent clergy and lay members of the churches, of an over-all prayer committee with both men and women's divisions, and area committees, and district committees, each with its own responsibility.

Time was purchased on a fifty-thousand-watt station at twelve-fifteen Monday through Friday. The program slogan became "Noontime is prayer time." Each day team members would read a message and make known the prayer needs of the crusade.

Cottage prayer leaders would hold their meetings for a further thirty minutes of solemn supplication.

A letter offered this advice:

"Hold the first prayer meeting on April 1 in your home or place of business and invite your neighbors or business associates.

"From day to day try to arrange a prayer meeting in different homes in your neighborhood.

"Distribute our prayer topic cards to each home in your neighborhood.

"Keep your prayer meetings informal. They are not to be dress-up affairs.

"Neighbors, friends, or business associates who cannot meet with your group should be asked to tune in the 'Prayer Time' broadcast at 12:15 P.M. and conduct their own prayer meetings in their own way."

People have asked, "Why does Graham need a year or more for his team to prepare a crusade? What do they do?"

Moving millions of prayers to God is one of the things. In numbers and in intensity, they are quite without precedent.

Two months before the crusade Haymaker told the executive committee that every postal zone in New York had a wide-awake prayer organization.

Already, three thousand local prayer groups were meeting daily.

Organizations in thirty-nine foreign countries had cabled that they were praying for New York.

Over eight thousand individual prayer partners had pledged their support in New York alone.

As time passed, the big map in Haymaker's office became covered with letters and cables from all parts of the globe.

From Pakistan . . . "We are joining others around the world in prayer for the crusade."

From Hong Kong . . . "I wish you could hear the prayers of God's people in this part of the world for you folks in New York."

From Cairo, Egypt . . . "Our people pray expressly for your success each morning at 7 A.M. May the power of the Holy Spirit give you strength."

From Mexico . . . "There is a group here in Mexico City which is lifting you and your team up in prayer. Be assured of our wholehearted support."

From London . . . "We're with you continuously in prayer, believing that God can change the course of world history through this crusade."

There were so many others. . . .

Over thirty groups were meeting in Formosa alone, with Madame Chiang Kai-shek and her close friends comprising one unit.

All-night prayer meetings were being held in five different cities in India.

And surely the most bizarre prayer group in history was meeting in Japan. It was composed exclusively of convicts who had been condemned to death. An American missionary had organized it in the death house of a Japanese prison. Those men, with no hope of their own, prayed that there might be hope in the lives of New Yorkers.

By May 14, the day of the Service of Dedication in the Garden, crusade headquarters had responded to requests for 250,000 prayer cards.

Now 10,000 local prayer groups were meeting daily.

That night, people living in 105 countries would be praying for New York.

That night ten great churches in metropolitan New York, one for each of the crusade's ten borough and suburban communities, would stay open from dusk till dawn to accommodate the thousands who had pledged to attend.

In Montreat, Billy Graham already knew the weight of those prayers, and had sensed that great things were in the making. Beginning his crusade, their power lent strength when it was needed. There is a diary entry for May 23, which closes with these significant words:

"Came back to the room . . . and was so tired that I lay down for half an hour. However, there has been one strange and wonderful thing thus far in the campaign. Though I have had great reason to be tired, yet I have had a basic strength that I don't think I've felt before. I think this is largely from the overwhelming prayer support we are receiving from around the world. I also have an inner peace and relaxation that I have not felt in a long time. I have taken this as from God, and give him praise for it."

Leighton Ford, young Presbyterian minister from Canada, was director of ministerial relations. His job was to place the crusade story before every Protestant pastor in metropolitan New York. It was an impossible, superhuman assignment.

Where does a person start? In other cities the point of origin was a list. One wrote letters, one made calls.

But no one in New York, no denomination, no organization, had such a list. To be sure, there was a directory of big strong churches, but nothing of the kind for all the others.

Ford pitched in with the energy and skill that had once made him the youngest Youth for Christ Director in the U.S.A. or Canada. Charles Riggs, who had served in other crusades as a director of counseling and follow-up, stepped in to help.

They began to call on ministers, door to door and parsonage to parsonage. It soon became apparent that two men or twenty men could not do the gigantic job properly.

Riggs joked, "This thing is bigger than both of us."

"We'll get the best list we can and write everybody letters," Ford decided.

By dividing the city into nine areas, by appointing a chairman for each, they began to uncover whole coveys of missing ministers. Hundreds were the pastors of so-called store-front churches, loosely organized congregations filling unoccupied stores, taking up collections to pay the rent, and moving on or closing up when the landlord found a better tenant.

Finally, their list had about three thousand names.

Their letters explained Graham's mission and the master crusade plan. They asked for a response from pastors who would designate members from their flocks to act as prayer partners, ushers, choristers, etc. . . .

Ford and Riggs visited each borough and every suburban community with a Protestant church council and made speeches. With each trip they learned that New York was bigger, more exhausting, more absorbing, and more challenging than any other metropolis in their experience.

They also learned about human nature. It will surprise some that ministers of the Gospel, in the main, are just like other people. They enjoy the comfort of the way of life to which they are accustomed. Imagine being the vicar of a pleasant parish, with a happy congregation and a balanced budget. Imagine having your study suddenly invaded by an onslaught of such letters, cards, telegrams—and perhaps persons—as had never crossed your ecclesiastical path. Imagine coming face to face with a vibrant, zealous, burning young man who beseeches you to lend your weight to the Christian effort of evangelism, who refuses to take "no" for an answer until both of you have asked God's guidance in a prayer that can have only one ending, your total capitulation.

Such a situation might seem to be overdrawn. "Oh, the lethargy of God's people," the young evangelists sighed a thousand times.

Some denominations were, in the beginning, noticeably slow to join up. Graham often made flying visits to meet their representatives at luncheon gatherings.

But in the end, approximately fifteen hundred pastors and churches were solidly behind the crusade. From them there came the sturdy phalanxes of volunteers who gave muscles and sinews to the organizational skeleton that was supplied by the Graham team.

Walter H. Smyth, of Bethesda, Maryland, was director of Group Reservations. When delegations from 112 churches came and went happily on the opening night, he breathed a vast sigh of relief. His patrons were pleased.

Not so a newspaperman who had counted the reserved seats. "Between your delegations from churches, ushers, choir, and counselors, you use about nine thousand seats," he challenged. "Wouldn't you call that 'packing' the house?"

Smyth said, "We have two missions. First, to reach the unchurched, for whom we have ten thousand seats. Second, to strengthen the churches. If nine thousand church people enjoy Christian fellowship night after night, listen to Dr. Graham's sermons and rededicate themselves, I think that's a good thing, too."

He could have told him about "Operation Andrew," but a phone call came from a desperate bus driver. "This traffic! And I had to get a flat tire," he said. "We'll be late. Can you hold them seats?"

"How many?"

"Fifty."

"Get here as soon as you can."

It happened every night. "My motor's conked but we'll get there!" "We're outa gas!" "A lady just fainted from the heat. We'll be delayed, but please hold our places."

George Cornell, whose Associated Press stories gave all America a clear picture of Garden events, explained Operation Andrew early in June.

"One person brings another," he wrote.

"It's called Operation Andrew—derived from the fact that the Apostle Andrew brought his brother Peter to Jesus."

"Very few ever came to Jesus without somebody bringing them," Graham says.

There are some striking examples:

He told of Jack L. Lewis, Jewish-born New York businessman who was led to Christianity by members of the team, reserving a box and filling it with fifteen to eighteen friends each night, many of whom made decisions. And of General John Reed Kilpatrick, president of the Garden, reserving *two* boxes instead of the one he holds regularly for all other events, and bringing famous guests such as General Albert Wedemeyer, Perle Mesta, Diana Barrymore, and Mrs. Alfred Gwynne Vanderbilt.

The largest metropolitan delegation consisted of 2500 members of the Saint George Association, a group of municipal employees. Another 2000 came from the Abyssinian Baptist Church in Harlem.

The largest group from out of town came by special train from Lancaster, Pennsylvania. The most distant point represented was Louisville, Kentucky, which sent two separate trainloads.

Governor Frank G. Clement of Tennessee led 910 from Nashville, Tennessee, on a three-day visit. Over 400 came from Michigan. Special trains ran from Atlanta and other southern cities.

One unforgettable troop paraded up Broadway and into the Garden behind its young conductor, who had thoughtfully equipped himself with a surplus army command speaker. The instructions he gave his motley army were surely heard in heaven.

A Virginia delegation of four hundred arrived aboard a special train one morning with what they called a "hymn-singing hangover." The party left Richmond the previous night on a train that included a chapel car. The railway company had created it by removing the tables from a diner and installing an electric organ. During the nine hours of the overnight trip, six Richmond pastors conducted services in rotation. Old-fashioned religious hymns were sung chain-style. "Suddenly we looked out and it was broad daylight," one visitor mused.

An auto caravan that motored to Manhattan sent a substantial contribution on its return home. They wrote Graham, "We all slept in our cars after hearing your sermon. The money we saved is our contribution to your great work."

84

But the chief burden of organizing delegations and bringing others was carried by the people of the churches. By the hundreds, they knocked on doors and wrote letters of invitation. One man in a New York apartment went from floor to floor ringing doorbells. Although he knew none of his neighbors in the beginning, before the crusade was half over, he had brought almost forty to the Garden, and half of these had made decisions.

Many ministers brought their own flocks night after night, reserving a bus on faith that it would be filled. One pastor who conducted a group of forty-five young people reported that all of them went forward. And afterward they passed their counseling literature to the bus driver, and he made a decision, too.

An Operation Andrew decision that was especially gratifying came through some Hi-BA kids. One of their senior friends was a top-notch young scientist and a practicing atheist. Being widely read, he gave his fellow students a hard time. After much persuasion he joined a bus party with forty others. When the kids sang hymns he tried to get off. At the Garden the smirk left his face and he became strangely quiet. When the invitation came, every Hi-BA member bowed, praying hard. He sat there, expressionless. Graham stopped the music and said, "I feel there is someone here tonight to whom God is speaking. I feel he is almost persuaded. We'll wait a moment. So come now! There's plenty of time. Get right up and come."

The boy slid to the edge of his seat, rose to his feet, took the long, hard first step, and then marched forward like a man who knew exactly where he was going.

A club chartered a bus for a May service. Among the guests invited was Rosemary, a high-school junior. She was a rough, tough girl, very popular, especially with the boys. That night the ride to New York City was full of pleasant joking and hymn singing. Rosemary joined in when she knew the words. When Graham issued the invitation for inquirers to come forward, Rosemary got to her feet and ran eagerly all the way to the front. After that night she became a diligent student of the Bible and joined a church. Before the crusade ended she brought fifteen of her old gang to the foot of the Cross.

A counselor reported this result of Operation Andrew . . . "Georgia is a twenty-two-year-old office worker in New York. She had no connections with any church. One day someone in her office announced that a group would be going to the meeting. Having nothing else to do, she joined the group.

"For the first time in her life, she heard the Gospel presented clearly, positively, authoritatively. And she responded. Her conversion was a very definite experience. In fact, it was so thorough that within one week she succeeded in bringing her closest friend to the crusade, who also made a decision for Christ. Georgia reported this to me as we sat within sight of her friend as she was being counseled.

" 'I now hope that I can win all of my family,' she said. 'And at the office we have set aside a daily time for prayer.' "

At the crusade's end Smyth flew to San Francisco to speak to ministers planning to support Graham's first 1958 crusade. He had an urgent message. "A pastor gets out of a crusade what he puts into it. Don't wait until public interest or enthusiasm forces you to organize bus parties and auto caravans. Begin with the first meeting! If all New York pastors had worked in the beginning as they came to do toward the end, there would be no counting the extra souls saved or the rededications among their congregations."

The TV program called "Impact" was another team effort. Telecast from Station WPIX-TV at eleven-thirty each night, it said, in effect, "If you're troubled, give us a call. Here's our number. Jesus Christ can help." At the other end of the line, counselors waited.

A call came one night from a lady with a cultivated voice. She was married and had two children. "I cannot keep one of the commandments," she said. "It is the one about honoring my father and my mother."

The counselor asked her to get a Bible. She had none. "Then why don't we pray?" The woman began to sob. "Can I see you to talk more about this?" she asked. The counselor invited her to lunch next day, and with a Bible between them in a crowded restaurant, she led the unhappy woman to a decision for Christ.

A call came from a railway man whose wife and daughter had already been converted at the Garden. Now they were out of the house and he had "just forty-six minutes" to get things straightened out. With fourteen and a half minutes to go, he made his decision. Later he called back again to ask if he could refer his wife to the

86

"Impact" office, "otherwise she'll never believe me." Amazingly, he was a spare-time church organist. He had listened to preaching every Sunday for forty years, but this was the first time it had reached his heart.

A woman phoned whose problem was acute alcoholism. "I have a craving for liquor that is uncontrollable," she said. "My husband is good, we have a new home, there's plenty of money. Yet I'm destroying everything I want to hold onto."

The counselor told her the hard facts: "Take Jesus into your heart as Savior. Let him take command. You will then want to get rid of every drop of liquor, dismiss your drinking friends, and set new standards in your home."

Then they prayed and the woman asked Christ to clean her house and save her soul. Later she was introduced to a live Christian church.

Mel Dibble, producer and master of ceremonies, is a Baptist evangelist who joined the team for the summer. Once a TV performer dangerously close to alcoholism, he had been led to Christ by Graham several years ago and then turned to full-time Christian work.

"We get the loners, the people in hotels, the drunks, the barroom girls," he said. "'Impact' was designed to be heard when regular church people are in bed."

A counseling session was no passing matter to the fourteen counselors who took calls each night. Each referred to the Bible generously to relate a caller's problem to God's Word. Always, there was prayer together. Finally, there was the penitent's prayer, the same employed by the Reverend Joe Blinco in the counseling room at the Garden, which the counselor led and the caller repeated.

Always, an effort was made to get each new Christian into a church. Sometimes the more immediate problem was one of preventing murder or of saving the life of a person who had lost all reason for living. A calypso dancer who blamed her misery on a hapless marriage had been ready to kill her husband until she responded to "Impact's" guidance. Many nights the telephones were busy until two or three o'clock in the morning.

The "Impact" harvest, so far as it could be measured, was 566 newborn souls.

The team member seen by the public more than any other was Cliff Barrows. Raised in California, educated at Bob Jones University, he moved with Graham through the Youth for Christ movement into mass evangelism.

In the military, he would be described as a man who wears a half-dozen caps.

He led the choir, rehearsing it for a half hour each night before the crusade service.

He produced Graham's weekly "Hour of Decision" broadcast.

He produced the daily "Prayer-time" program on WABC.

He often appeared on "Impact," the nightly TV program of the crusade.

He saw to the recording on tape of all Graham's sermons.

He was platform manager at each Garden service, and Yankee Stadium and Times Square, greeting the audience, welcoming delegations, and making announcements.

He was, in effect, the master of ceremonies for every TV-cast that extended Madison Square Garden into millions of homes.

But what no audience could see was his electronic partnership with Graham, by which he controlled the almost invisible wire that connected the evangelist's necktie mike with the loud-speaker system. When Billy first used such a mike in 1949 his long legs frequently got tangled. Barrows said, "I can fix it." Seating himself two dozen feet behind the evangelist, he held the wire in his fingers, playing it out like an angler. Graham could roam the stage at will, with no skein of copper hobbling his strides. It worked like that in New York except for one additional feature. The pulpit was equipped with two red lights. It was Barrows' job to signal when the allotted time was almost up. The sixty-second light was his final warning to Graham to finish his remarks.

The esteem in which he was held is in such reports as these:

From a Jersey mother . . . "The fellowship of Mr. Barrows is something I cannot explain. I've never been able to shake hands with him, but just hearing him pray and talk to us the way he does, I feel that I know him and he knows me."

From an Episcopalian . . . "Sitting out front, I found that I wanted to work with Mr. Barrows, whose personality was so appealing. I felt as if I couldn't stand it if I didn't help sing 'How Great Thou Art.'"

From a Baptist . . . "I have enjoyed the deep spiritual direction of Cliff Barrows. Surely this man is touched by the power of God."

From a Manhattan chorister . . . "What amazing results he gets! So many ordinary voices, so many coming and going, yet he whips us into shape. He is a bona fide genius."

From a faithful grandmother . . . "I feel real sorry for those who had to sit out front. They were missing the best part of the service, the little prayers that Cliff Barrows said each time we finished a rehearsal."

Patricia Campion, late of London, joined the Graham team in New York to evangelize the "up-and-outers." To the uninitiated, these are the opposite of the "down-and-outers." In the history of evangelism, they are the hardest of all sinners to reach.

Miss Campion's background was useful and interesting. Brought up in a formally religious home, she rejected God and became interested in Britain's Young Communist League. At twenty, she was a promising student at the Royal Academy of Drama and Music, and well on her way to becoming a Red.

One evening in 1954 she heard of a young evangelist who was preaching at an ice rink called Harringay. She and some friends went over to see if they could pick up a few theatrical pointers. Instead, they learned about God.

In full-time religious work, she came to New York to invade the drawing rooms of society, and to tell a story so ancient that few of her acquaintances had heard it. At luncheons, teas, and potluck parties, she talked about Jesus Christ.

Three lovely ladies dined with her one evening. They were gowned by Hattie Carnegie and shod by Delman, but they wanted something they saw in Pat.

"Where do you get such radiant power?" one asked.

"Come to the Garden and I'll show you," Miss Campion said.

This woman, a beautiful Californian who is now a member of the Connecticut country-club set, accepted her invitation. And presently, old friends were saying to her: "What has happened to you? You're so different."

She said, "I found Jesus Christ and he has transformed my life."

During the next months, three close friends and her mother, who came for a visit, all joined her in going forward at the Garden.

The second woman at that dinner was the wife of a successful architect. About twenty-eight, she was the mother of three. Raised in a Christian home, she had never heard of the new birth. "Aren't you a Christian because your parents are Christians? How else does one become a Christian?"

In the Garden, she found her way.

The third dinner guest was a self-sufficient, matter-of-fact woman who was raising a large and successful family. She told Miss Campion, "I have everything I need. Do you mean to tell me that I can be still happier?"

When they went to the Garden, the message she heard tore away her ego and self-assurance, and she, too, joined the parade of inquirers. With some guidance, she began to read her Bible, to find herself useful in a church, and suddenly life opened up around her in a way she had not thought possible. "Now when I pray," she said, "I look up, not down."

That was only one dinner with the up-and-outers, but each of those women brought dozens of guests to other services, and their guests brought more guests, and so the widening ripples spread.

Paul E. Little was the team member assigned to extend the crusade to every college campus. It was a difficult assignment. Little's checkup showed two hundred thousand students and fifty colleges, plus forty schools of nursing.

One obstacle was the atmosphere of intellectual skepticism found on most campuses. So many undergraduates nowadays exalt modern science at the expense of faith in God.

Graham knew this well, because he spoke for a strenuous week in the early spring at Yale University. He had a story for their intellectuals that illustrated the dilemma of science.

A small boy came to visit a great astronomer at his observatory and saw his huge telescope. "How many stars can you see through that thing?" the boy asked.

"Well, if you put the figure '1' down, and follow it with twenty-three zeros, that's the number we can see."

The boy asked, "Gee, where'd they all come from?"

The professor said, "Well, they come from dust up there that kind of had an explosion."

"Wow! where did all that dust come from?"

90

"Oh, that dust came from the molecules that were up there once."

"Well, where did the molecules come from, sir?"

"Why, they came from atoms."

"Where did the atoms come from?"

"Well, son, they came from the neutrons that were all out there."

"Gee, where did the neutrons come from, Doc?"

"Oh, they came from a big burst of radiation."

The little fellow said, "Now tell me, sir, where did that big burst of radiation come from?"

"Go 'way from me, boy! You bother me!" the scientist screamed.

Graham added, "Science had reached the end of its rope. That's about all science can tell anyone about the universe."

On the premise that nobody can intellectualize his way into heaven, Graham sought to reach as many students as possible with his message of salvation produced by faith. The first thing Little organized was a mail campaign.

Letters went out to the presidents of every fraternity offering speakers, members of the famous Graham team, for fraternity-house discussions and the free use of a full-length crusade motion picture.

Representatives were appointed on every campus.

Students were recruited for counselor training.

Posters and handbills were distributed announcing a Student's Night at the Garden on May 18, 1957.

Publicity stories were written for papers at Columbia University, New York University, Adelphi, and many other institutions.

A three-day lecture series was held on many campuses.

Finally it was May 18 and College Night at the Garden. Over twenty-one hundred students came in delegations from forty-four institutions. Famous colleges were represented: Yale, West Point, N. Y. U., Princeton, Columbia, Cornell, Rutgers, Vassar. . . . So were smaller, more specialized schools: Brooklyn Polytechnic, Cooper Union, Hofstra, Montclair State Teachers, Stevens Institute, Wagner College, Newark College of Engineering, a dozen schools of nursing, among many others.

Later there were study groups, weekend conferences, and picnic suppers for those who made decisions. The invitation read: What to bring? Sports clothes, blanket, Bible.

All through the summer it was a time of harvest. A student

came to a team member after a service. Big, blond, smiling, he put out his hand. "I'm a Rutgers man. Tonight I accepted Christ," he said.

"How do you know you are saved?" he was asked.

"I feel it here." The student pounded his chest. "Besides, the Bible says so."

Little told of a second-year medical student. "His head was crammed with ancient and modern philosophies. He cleared the cobwebs out of his thinking one night by accepting Christ. It was amazing to watch him change. He was so excited about his experience that he brought his wife, who made a decision, and then his sister."

A special effort was made to reach the ten thousand foreign students in New York, many of whom were from countries which prohibit the entry of Christian missionaries. Through International Students, Inc., these foreign intellectual leaders of the future were brought to many services both at the Garden and at Manhattan's famous International House.

At least a score of Moslems, Hindus, and Buddhists made definite decisions.

A student from Guatemala stopped in New York on the way home from Arkansas University. She visited the Garden and was greatly moved. Before she sailed for home, where her brother is a Jesuit priest, she accepted Jesus Christ.

An Arab boy, whose parents were devout Moslems, had never found his religion satisfying. At the Garden he made a decision. Returning to his campus, he called a meeting of fellow Moslems to tell them his discovery of Christianity.

A man from Persia, a worshiper of the sun, a Zoroastrian, had never seen or read any portion of the Bible. He came to the Garden as a lark. But he listened to the evangelist and went forward to make a decision.

Chiang Yee was a Chinese student at a technical institute. All his life he had observed the strict moral teachings of Confucius. The words he heard at the Garden persuaded him that the Christian way was better. He went forward with other inquirers, and later sent four members of his family toward the same goal.

Any of these might be world leaders tomorrow. One American boy who almost certainly will lead many other Americans, wrote this letter to Dr. Graham from the United States Military Academy at West Point.

"I came forward and gave my life to Christ at your July 2 meeting, and I have never done a wiser thing. I am deeply sorry that I'll be unable to attend your final meeting. We cadets are not permitted to leave the post. What a fool is a man who does not know of the strength and peace God can give him if he would only seek it. This, and other truths, I have learned. I thank you, as I thank God, for making this possible."

At the crusade's end, Paul Little counted up his sheep. Of firm decisions, he found 2,328.

Lane Adams was another of those thin-hipped, six-foot evangelists on the Graham team.

His assignment was show business.

His background? He had been a navy fighter pilot, a singer, and a night-club entertainer.

When Graham asked him to join the New York crusade staff, he was a ministerial student at Columbia Theological Seminary in Georgia, just three months from graduation. He left school, said good-bye to wife and child, and arrived in Manhattan on March 21.

As he was walking up neon-lighted Broadway, the enormity of the challenge struck home. How could one penetrate this false front of glitter, garish billboards, and make-believe merriment?

So far as Adams knows, he was the first Protestant missioner to explore the jungles of Times Square. Like Dr. Livingstone, Judson, and other eminent missionaries, he looked about for allies. Where, he wondered, were the Christians.

He found a handful. These gave him a few phone numbers, introduced him to their friends. Saint Paul newly arrived in Antioch or Ephesus must have followed a similar course.

One day, he told an editor of *Variety*, the show-business weekly, that evangelist Graham intended to fill Madison Square Garden for six midsummer weeks. The story was printed, front page, about Graham's evangelical showmanship, and about Lane Adams' mission. The Graham box-office record was published. A buzz of interest rose from the Rialto.

Much of the talk was, "This Graham is crazy. Nobody can fill eighteen thousand seats a night this summer. Who're his stars?"

Adams said, "Our star is Jesus Christ."

People who met the intent young man came away with the feeling that perhaps, just perhaps, there might be a miracle at the Garden.

Early, it became apparent that Christian actors, writers, and entertainers needed a meeting place. Overwhelmed numerically by those who held alien creeds, they required the nourishment of fellowship. A luncheon was planned to see what others might think. Billy Graham arranged his schedule to attend. Between thirty and forty were expected. Reservations came from seventy-five.

That was the beginning of New York's Christian Arts Fellowship with Metropolitan Opera basso Jerome Hines as president.

Hines assumed his role gladly. "We have two objectives," he said. "First, evangelism. We mean bringing people to a point of total surrender and commitment. Second, fellowship. We mean the establishment of interpersonal relationships for the purpose of aiding one another in spiritual growth. This group must not degenerate into one that merely puts on plays. We must witness by our lives."

The fellowship was growing at the crusade's end, and had scheduled regular meetings.

A newsman asked Adams, "How did you know what to do to set up your program?"

He replied, "First, I prayed for guidance. Then I located Christians, one at a time. I tried to inspire them to reach out to others and testify for Christ."

"This is a busy town. Did anybody co-operate?"

Lane said, "The co-operation was phenomenal. People were thirsting for the spirit. After a phone call or a personal talk, they would end up at the Garden. If they had questions or reservations, they lost them there. So many called me back and said, "This is the greatest experience in my whole life."

Millions have seen the pretty faces of blond twins who appear on a popular TV program. Singly but supported by the prayers of workers in the show-business group, they went to the Garden and gave their hearts to God.

A young man came into Adams' office one day—he thought he

was calling on a booking agency that had recently occupied the space—and asked if there were any bookings for him.

"There sure are," Adams told him. "Tonight at the Billy Graham Crusade in Madison Square Garden."

The young man accepted the unexpected invitation. That night he became a Christian.

Sometimes a phone call had unexpected results. For days Adams tried to reach a famous TV producer. His secretary repeatedly stated that the executive was not available. "Is there anything I can do?" she asked.

"Yes," he said. "I have a reserved-seat ticket for the Billy Graham service that I hoped he would want. Would you be able to use it?"

"I've been reading about Billy Graham," she said. "I think I'd like to hear him."

So another inquirer made her way to the Garden and a personal decision to live for Christ.

Americans are generally reluctant to discuss their religious experiences. For most, religion is a comforting cloak; not a platform for speechmaking. Graham and Adams preached that a Christian has no choice but to testify both by word and deed.

"Bring somebody with you tomorrow night," Graham exhorted his audiences.

"Find a friend and take him to hear Billy Graham," Adams told every person he met.

The consequences are sometimes hard to believe.

One young Christian in show business brought a celebrated actor, a hardened sinner whose notorious immorality had titillated Broadway for seventeen years. Unexpectedly, the words of Graham's first sermon got beneath his skin. He returned night after night, fourteen nights in a row. Finally, with it all straight in his mind, he calmly made his decision.

But this was not enough. From that day forward he became a fervent tireless worker. The tally of those who found Christ because of him will probably never be known, but there were thirty-six who were led by him into the Garden.

That is the secret of a Graham crusade, if there is one. It has worked since the beginning of time. One man brings another.

The team method of evangelism has been criticized so often

that Graham sometimes feels the need to prove its validity. One night at the Garden, in mid-sermon, he mentioned an editorial in the Charlotte *Observer*. "It shows that the Apostle Paul used a team when he left Jerusalem to establish churches in the cities around the Mediterranean. I'm going to get it and read it to you," he said delightedly.

Here it is:

"If Billy Graham needs any defense against those who object to his evangelistic work because they do not approve of his 'organized methods,' he can surely turn to St. Paul," the *Observer* commented. "When Paul decided to evangelize that den of iniquity, Ephesus, he did not go at once. Instead, he sent two advance agents, Aquila and Priscilla, who had two years of experience in Corinth and before that in Rome. Their job was to organize the campaign and soften up Ephesus for the main event when Paul arrived.

"They were helped by a brilliant young man from Alexandria named Apollos—the kind of orator who could make an audience eat out of his hand—who did much of the softening-up work after Aquila and Priscilla corrected his doctrinal errors.

"Then came Paul, not alone but accompanied by professionals, Timothy, Luke, and others, all of whom had been through the mill, fought with mobs, and spent some days and nights in prison.

"From the names mentioned in the Epistles and in Acts in connection with the Ephesus campaign, it can be estimated that Paul had a team of about twenty persons, all experts, who knew their way around the business of evangelism.

"If Billy Graham has too much organization, he has excellent precedents."

11

The crusade's mission was to reach the unchurched, so Graham preached in the Garden, preached in suburbs, and fought New York's indifference with zeal and Scripture . . .

The Billy Graham New York Crusade set at least two special records.

It achieved the longest, broadest and deepest co-operation between evangelist, team members, pastors, churches, and congregations in recent evangelistic experience.

It gave Billy Graham's six-foot-two physique the longest, toughest marathon course of outside meetings, Gospel rallies, and mobile warfare against Beelzebub of his career.

Let it be understood that these pious attacks on the unchurched did not all spring full-panoplied from the brows of the evangelistic team. Greater New York's own "newborn"—clergy, priests, and presbyters—are both able and inventive. Their proposals were among the most useful of the weird and wonderful excursions required of Dr. Graham.

"And they went forth and preached everywhere, the Lord working with them, and confirming the word with signs following," so reads the twentieth verse of Mark 16.

That was written almost two thousand years ago, but it remains a perfect description of the New York Crusade as it burst through the Garden's walls.

And they—Billy Graham and the members of his team—went forth and preached everywhere. . . .

Hereafter, in approximate chronology, is a chronicle of three amazing months, with their trials and errors and even a few hints at human frailty.

It began four days after his successful opening in the Garden. It began with a hoarse, weary Graham going to the borough of Brooklyn.

So his adventure began, in his own words:

"Went to Leif Ericson Square in Brooklyn this afternoon. It was the first experience I ever had preaching in Brooklyn. Forty thousand people were there. It was Norwegian Independence Day. I preached the Gospel and asked those that would like to receive Christ to lift their hands. And hundreds responded.

"The Norwegians were wonderful. They were dressed in their old country, colorful clothes. They had a parade, and then the service. This was the largest New York crowd that it has been my privilege to address. Interest seems to be growing everywhere.

"Mr. Erling Olsen brought us back from Leif Ericson Square, and I went immediately to bed. I was very hoarse as a result of the open-air preaching. I was deeply concerned that my throat would not be up to preaching tonight. I was also concerned over the fact that this was the first Sunday-night service that we have had in this country in many years. We did not know how it would work out. We had had no seats reserved in advance for tonight, and it was on a first come, first served basis. I felt that Madison Square Garden would be only about half filled. When we arrived at seven twenty-five, the doors were already locked. Jerry says that tonight there were almost twenty thousand in the Garden and hundreds were turned away.

"Cliff, I thought, did the most wonderful job directing the music tonight, yet. The choir sang along with Beverly Shea 'How Great Thou Art.' I love that song. So many of our songs are to ourselves: 'Revive Us Again,' 'Oh, How I Love Jesus.' But here it is toward God, 'How Great Thou Art.' Then the choir sang 'The Lord's Prayer' by Malotte. Cliff turned around and had the entire congregation of almost twenty thousand people sing the climax. What a thrill! I saw some of the old Christians wiping tears from their eyes. How many of those Christians had long been praying for this day when revival would come back to New York. Where sin abounds, grace does much more abound. One of the reasons we came to New York is that we felt it needed it more than most places. There are fewer Christians here. I feel that God would have us to go to hard places, not the easy ones!

"Preached on 'The End of the World,' using the story of Noah. Had great liberty, did not feel bound by my hoarse throat. They started streaming forward before I was even through the invitation. I am sure that something like a thousand came forward tonight. It was by far the greatest response we have seen yet. Certainly God is moving mightily. The promise of the Lord rings in my ears as I go to bed: 'Fear not, nor be dismayed; tomorrow go out against them, for the Lord will be with you!'"

Two days later he made an important appearance before New York's famous Dutch Treat Club, whose membership includes many of the world's greatest men in the field of creative arts. In his audience were such "names" as Lowell Thomas, Samuel Hopkins Adams, Roy Howard, and Bruce Barton. He told them:

"We don't have any hope for the future any more. The capacity to depopulate the world is in our hands. And somebody could use it."

He saw Father Keller among his audience, which recalled a story he had heard from the Catholic leader in New Orleans. It concerned a meeting at night when the electric power in a great stadium was turned off. One match was lighted, then another and another, until a hundred thousand matches had been lighted. Graham said, "I'll light my match. You light yours. Together, we can light up the whole world."

He came wondering how he could impress these "intellects" with his simple message, but as he spoke he realized that they, like so many others of the world's leaders, had no answer either. He flung his positive Gospel at them, provoking their attention. "With all your power, if you would do all you could to help change people," he said, "then the world might be saved from blowing itself apart. I believe that Christ can change a man's life. A few dedicated men can do it."

His final challenge was, "If you know of any better way, go to it."

The club, applauding, gave him its rarest tribute, a rising vote of thanks.

The newsstands suddenly blossomed with copies of *Newsweek*, his picture on the cover above the blurb: "The Billy Graham 'Invasion'—Finally the Big One—'Save New York.'" In a special religious report, it said, "This week the man who had electrified London, Glasgow, Seattle and a dozen smaller cities of the world brought his high-voltage evangelism to the world's biggest city. His mission was to 'save New York.'"

Thus, one of the most widely distributed misconceptions of the crusade gained national currency. It stemmed from the word "saved." Graham had said, "I can save nobody. Only God saves." His hope, which he reiterated often, was, "that lives will be changed. If enough lives are changed, then society will be changed."

That week he and Ruth went to a Father's Day luncheon at the Waldorf-Astoria and sat at the head table with several other celebrities.

His diary reported: "We went to the Father's Day Luncheon at the Waldorf-Astoria. Senator McClellan of Arkansas, whom I had known for a number of years, was made Father of the Year. I had the privilege of accepting the award as the Father of the Year in the field of religion. I had the opportunity of meeting and talking to such celebrities as Mickey Mantle, the great baseball player. I sat down beside him and engaged him in some conversation, but he did not seem to be very talkative. I think he is terribly shy, with that country-come-to-town look. I hope he always keeps it. Certainly he is a great All-American boy. I invited him to the meetings and he said he hoped to come.

"Ruth and I sat at the head table. On one side of us were Mr. and Mrs. Charles Van Doren, whose name has become a household word because of his fantastic knowledge on a TV quiz program, and his father and mother were on the other side. We also met Mr. and Mrs. John Kelly, the parents of Grace Kelly, now the Princess of Monaco. When I made my speech I told them that I did not deserve the honor nearly so much as my wife, who had to be both father and mother to our children. I tried to remind them that our homes in America are in danger of breaking, and that we need to get back to the biblical concept of the meaning of the home. I told them of my own Christian home and the fact that we had Bible reading and prayer daily. I suggested that one of the reasons we have the breakdown in our homes is that we have neglected the principles and rules governing marriage that God laid down in the Bible."

That afternoon, resting in his hotel room, he received a telephone call that left him reinvigorated.

"Felt led to preach on 'The Heart' tonight. Spent an hour and a half in preparation," he wrote. "Dr. Norman Vincent Peale called me and said that people were praying wherever he had gone throughout the country, and informing me that he would be in the service tonight to pronounce the benediction. He is such a

Within these canyons of Wall Street, police estimated that a lunch-time crowd of 30,000 listened to evangelist Graham on July 10. Facing Broad Street and speaking from the steps of Federal Hall (*the pillared building to the right*), Graham stood on historic ground where George Washington had once been sworn in as the nation's first President. In the immediate left foreground is the banking house of J.P. Morgan & Co., then the sunlit Stock Exchange. In the extreme background is Trinity Church. Pointing to its spire-tipped cross, the evangelist called it a symbol of "the loving sacrifice of God in giving His only begotten Son to save the world." Sitting on the dais were George Champion, president of the Chase Manhattan Bank; Edwin Chinlund, treasurer of R.H. Macy & Co.; and Roger Hull, executive vice-president of the Mutual Life Insurance Co. of New York.

No living human ever saw such a sight on Broadway. Armistice celebrations and New Year's high jinks paled in comparison to the wall-to-wall carpet of humanity that stretched from Times Square and Forty-second Street southward as far as the eye could see. These photos, taken an hour before meeting time, were too early to catch the hosts that overflowed into cross streets. Speaking of Times Square, Graham said, "Tonight for a few moments it is being turned into a great cathedral as a symbol of spiritual revival that is now in progress in America. Let us tell the whole world tonight that we Americans believe in God."

Music Director Cliff Barrows (*foreground on high podium*) "hand directs" the white-bloused, white-shirted 2,000-voice Crusade Choir that half circles him in Madison Square Garden. Of the ministry of music, Dr. Graham wrote in his diary, "When the choir sang 'The Lord's Prayer' by Malotte, Cliff turned around and had the entire congregration of people sing the climax. What a thrill! I saw some of the old Christians wiping tears from their eyes. How many of those Christians had long been praying for this day when revival would come to New York! One of the reasons we came to New York is that it needed it more than most places. I feel that God would have us go to hard places, not the easy ones."

gracious and courteous man. His emphasis and mine are somewhat different, but I have met a great many people helped by him. Basically, he knows and loves the Gospel. As a youth he had a genuine conversion experience. His wife is one of the most godly women Ruth and I have ever met. She has been head of the women's prayer groups of New York and has endeared herself to thousands of Christian women in this area. He told me that his two children are coming to the services every night and that one of them is singing in the choir."

On the night of May 24, the crusade broke through the Garden walls to a section of Forty-ninth Street. A packed house left hundreds of disappointed pilgrims milling about outside. Graham greeted them from atop a table.

He wrote: "Tonight I preached on Zacchaeus coming to Christ out of curiosity and finding salvation. The building was packed to capacity, and about two thousand people were in the street. I went out and preached to them, standing on a table, and people up in their apartments all around were looking down and listening. I saw a dog sitting in one of the windows and he looked as though he were listening more intently even than some of the people. It seems that the Spirit of God has charged the atmosphere so that even the animals are affected. People's hearts are being prepared in strange and unusual ways. We are hearing so many thrilling stories of outstanding and unusual conversions. Certainly it is the Lord's doing, and not ours."

Elsewhere, the plight of the up-and-outers has been described. They are the millionaire families who, isolated from reality by their wealth, have little knowledge of God's plan of salvation. Someone thought—team member or volunteer—that Graham's personal impact on this segment of the unchurched would be salutary, and planned accordingly.

Billy and Mrs. Graham were invited to lunch at a fabulous estate in Old Westbury, that citadel of plutocrats and pink teas.

The hostess was Jane Pickens Langley, famous singer of radio and posh cabarets, now a leader of North Shore society.

"What a beautiful home the Langleys have," he wrote. "Mr. Langley used to be the president of the New York Stock Exchange. Their home is early American, has a lovely swimming pool and beautiful grounds. They had chairs set up on the lawn for about two hundred people. They were expecting fifty for lunch and then about a hundred and fifty more to come at one-thirty. I had not realized it was such an elaborate affair, nor did I realize till I got there that I was to speak. People began to arrive about eleven-thirty . . . the Whitneys, the Vanderbilts, the Cushings, and many other names I had heard so often. Several people came up and said they had been in the meetings already and two said they had come forward to receive Christ as Savior.

"It was a gorgeous day and we ate outside. As soon as lunch was over, others began to arrive. We went to the door and met them as they came in. Then we went to the back yard for that meeting. Mrs. Langley introduced me, and I spoke for about twenty-five minutes, explaining what an evangelist was, what the objectives of our meetings were, and then I presented the Gospel that I preach. Afterward we had about thirty or forty minutes of questions. They dealt with everything from how we finance the meetings to did I think it necessary to believe that Jesus was God in order to be saved."

That night the crusade moved to another sports arena, the Forest Hills Tennis Stadium, for its first big out-of-the-Garden rally. To it, on this cool evening, busses chugged from Long Island, Brooklyn, and Queens. These were "Operation Andrew" delegations with their salting of sinners. Jammed subway trains, stopping at the Forest Hills station nearby, emitted hearty, singing crowds.

Graham wrote of that service:

"The meeting tonight was in one of the most beautiful, compact, little stadiums I have ever seen. I understand it had never been filled before, and the officials were somewhat excited about the possibilities. It seated about fourteen thousand. It had already turned cool. A chilly wind was blowing. There was hardly any place for people to park. Planes were flying low overhead. Mr. Erling Olsen made a call to the La Guardia Airport and they promised to redirect flights. We would see planes take off, and then suddenly pull up and away.

"The stadium was just about filled when we arrived. It was a thrilling meeting. I felt great liberty in preaching. The choir sang 'How Great Thou Art' and also 'The Lord's Prayer.' The stadium was filled and you could hear a pin drop at times. When the invitation was given, hundreds came down and stood in front. It was a moving sight to hear hundreds of people praying the sinner's prayer, asking Christ to come into their hearts."

Sunday nights were important to the evangelist. Always the Garden was packed. Frequently the proportion of men and teen-agers was greater than during week nights. To his Sunday sermon he tried to give his unstinted best.

On the evening of May 26 it was not easy.

"Stayed in bed all morning," he wrote, "due to a severe stomach upset and pounding headache. Must have eaten something that didn't agree with me. Even during my devotional period, I felt sick and nauseated. Ruth had missed her train the night before and remained over. What a joy and comfort she is—always encouraging. She says the right thing at the right time, never too much or too little.

"We went to lunch with Dr. and Mrs. Norman Vincent Peale at their apartment on Fifth Avenue. What a joy they are! I don't know any two people that radiate Christ any more than the Peales. Mrs. Peale has been the head of our women's prayer meetings in New York and has done a magnificent job. Margaret Peale sings in the choir. I heard that Dr. Peale spent almost the entire sermon this morning on the crusade. We had a wonderful conversation at the table and later in the living room, totally on spiritual things. I felt edified and spiritually refreshed after being with them. Certainly here is a family that lives Christ. He may get some criticism on his theological emphasis at times, but there is one thing certain —he lives it.

"Dr. and Mrs. Peale drove Ruth and me back to the New Yorker. I kissed Ruth good-bye and she left for Montreat. I won't see her for three weeks. In a few minutes I was already homesick for her. Everywhere I turned in the room I could see her.

"Went to the service and preached on the home. I did not feel like preaching because I was still suffering from the effects of my physical disorder. I have learned, however, there is a great difference between liberty and power. I had very little liberty but apparently there was power in the service. The building was filled to capacity and hundreds accepted the invitation.

"I had preached primarily to Christians and therefore asked the entire audience to stand and rededicate their lives to Christ. Many stood. I am always convinced that on such a night, probably more is accomplished than when I preach directly to sinners. If we could only get Christians to be Christians in the home! Someone asked George Whitefield about a certain man—if he was a Christian. He said, "I don't know. I haven't asked his wife." It's one thing to be a Christian in public; it's another thing to be a Christian in private. Certainly Christ should dominate our home life. In my opinion, the one answer to the problem of the home is Christ. The passage concerning Hezekiah is applicable today to the American people: 'Set thine house in order.' We need to set our houses in order."

A crusader's day is many things. It is elation and discouragement, slaps on the back and jealous stings. It is disappointment in a cherished person or project.

The issue of *Life* dated July 1 had Graham on the cover in preaching pose and an eight-page photographic essay on those who came forward in the crusade. Obviously, it could only scratch the surface. It said, "Billy Graham opened his New York Crusade in high hopes that it would 'soon be like a mighty river through the city.' But after 37 days of his 66-day stand in Madison Square Garden, the river had not been mighty. New Yorkers have talked surprisingly little about Billy—unlike his smash hits in London and Los Angeles. Though he has had good crowds, a good portion of them have come not from New York city—originally the prime target—but from the suburbs and even further away.

"The great bulk of Billy's hearers have been church members already. Of the New York area's six million non-churchgoers, about one in 40 has actually gone to the Garden. A *Life* spot check shows that of the 21,000 who have come forward at Billy's invitation to make 'decisions for Christ'—to become wholly and actively Christian—four-fifths belong to a church.

"However, the 4,000 unchurched people who have 'decided,' are, by any measure, a good number. Whether this is enough—and indeed, whether Graham's approach is enough—is debated by two outstanding religious leaders on page 92."

The debaters were Dr. Reinhold Niebuhr of Union Theological Seminary, and Dr. John Sutherland Bonnell, pastor of the Fifth Avenue Presbyterian Church.

The Niebuhr argument summarized the position of the vast majority of Graham critics. He said:

"The growing success of the evangelist, Billy Graham, and the crowds he draws to Madison Square Garden may be explained in terms of his undoubted gifts. This handsome, youthful, modest and obviously sincere evangelist is better than any evangelist of his kind in American history.

"But there are Christians who, while respecting Graham's personal honesty, have their reservations about mass evangelism. Its success depends upon oversimplifying every issue of life. This in turn means appeal to the Scripture in terms which negate all the achievements of Christian historical scholarship. Graham admits that success eluded him until he could say merely, 'The Bible says . . .' Such a formula of salvation must also be simple and not include any of life's many ambiguities.

"Thus Graham declares: 'Every human problem can be solved and every hunger satisfied and every potential can be fulfilled when a man encounters Jesus Christ and comes in vital relation to God in him.'

"Perhaps because these solutions are rather too simple in any age, but particularly so in a nuclear one with its great moral perplexities, such a message is not very convincing to anyone—Christian or not—who is aware of the continual possibilities of good and evil in every advance of civilization, every discipline of culture, and every religious convention. Graham offers Christian evangelism even less complicated answers than it has ever before provided."

The Bonnell argument summarized the attitudes of a large majority of Greater New York pastors and laymen. He said:

"Judging by the number of 'decisions for Christ' recorded up to the present we can assume that by the close of the crusade on July 21, there will be about 35,000 such decisions.

"How shall we evaluate these developments? Certain trends are already discernible.

"One. The greatest impact will be felt in the churches of New York. It may well be that most of the people going forward will be active members of New York churches rather than the unchurched. Now this is not something to be deplored. The spiritual life of many a New York church will be strengthened by the presence of these dedicated members.

"Two. The most readily discernible contribution is the creation of a spiritual climate favorable to religious decision. Several ministers have told me that prospective members within their own congregations on whom they have spent much time and effort without result came to an immediate and affirmative decision after attending one or more of the Graham meetings. They are now active church members.

"Three. Many persons who have attended the meetings at Madison Square Garden have been deeply impressed and not a few of them have, in their own hearts, rededicated themselves to Christ without going forward to the platform. I have talked with scores of such persons whose religious training and outlook kept them from this public demonstration of their inner resolve. There is good reason to believe that for every one who goes to the counseling room there are two others in the vast area who have made a new covenant with Christ."

Evangelist Graham, following a long-observed policy, made no public response. This was American journalism. Competent reporters looked at what they saw, photographed it, and told whatever truth they observed. His private grief was that so few members of the profession could understand from personal experience the significance and sweep of his mission.

Stung by *Life's* declaration, the executive committee authorized its chairman, Roger Hull, to set the record straight.

He wrote to *Life's* editors: "Since this article appeared, we have asked the people in the Garden who live or work in New York City to stand. Each night, as best we can judge, 80% to 85% of the audience indicate that they either live or work in New York City.

"The article implied that the Crusade has made no real impact on New York, such as was made on Los Angeles. In Los Angeles there were 3,000 total decisions with a total attendance of 280,000. Here in New York, decisions already exceed 28,000 and attendance is already well over 900,000."

Graham had expressed himself clearly enough the previous April before the National Association of Evangelicals in Buffalo, New York.

The *Evening News* reported these unabashed words:

"Some people do not believe with me theologically. In England they say that I am taking preaching back fifty years. I must plead guilty. I believe in the verbal inspiration of the Bible, the Virgin Birth, the vicarious atonement, and in the bodily resurrection of our Lord. But I don't disagree with the man who doesn't believe. I don't argue with him and try to make him believe the way I do.

"Some people just don't agree with evangelism in general. We don't fight back when a minister says he just can't agree with evangelism.

"Some people say that too much money is spent—a million dollars is being spent for the campaign in New York, but I have never heard those people criticize our government for spending many times that many millions on a fighting plane.

"Some people don't like our sponsorship [with reference to some fundamentalists who are critical because there were theological liberals among his sponsors]. The Apostle Paul went to services sponsored by a synagogue that didn't believe in the dignity of Christ. Paul was sponsored on another occasion by the heathen philosophers of Mars Hill. Let me make this very clear. I intend to go anywhere, any time, and be sponsored by anybody, if by so doing I can preach the Gospel of Jesus Christ without any strings attached. I will say with Whitefield that if I would be invited to preach a city-wide campaign in the Vatican, I'd do it!

"People do not agree with sending converts back to the churches of their choice. In the first place we don't call them converts. God converts and I don't know whether a man is converted or not. We like to call them inquirers. We have left this matter in the hands of the Holy Spirit.

"What do we expect from the New York Crusade? Well, Christ will be preached and souls will be saved. And any man who can't rejoice over the salvation of souls—I doubt his own conversion!"

And suddenly May was gone and June came in with a brand-new challenge, one that is discussed more fully in Chapter 12, but drawing from the evangelist an additional outpouring of strength and fire.

The *World-Telegram* noted it thus: "A man who refuses to quit when he's ahead, Billy Graham pits religion against show business tonight when his Madison Square Garden war with the devil makes its television debut . . . His opposition will be two of television's best—Perry Como and Jackie Gleason. Billy himself is all modesty. He doesn't give himself much of a chance to outdraw his two opponents and says he'll be satisfied 'if I get the leftovers.'"

This was also the day of the crusade's first official concern with racketeers. Canvassers were knocking on metropolitan doors, asking for contributions to help the Billy Graham Crusade, and apparently getting them. A warning was issued by the crusade office that any door-to-door solicitor was a phony.

A continuation of Niebuhr's disapproval was published in *Advance,* official magazine of the Congregational Christian Churches, where he wrote, "Working ministers are reduced to ballyhoo helpers in the effort to swell crowds. Their essential dignity is compromised as leaders of Christian congregations in which the Christian life is socially embodied."

Then he added:

"Graham honestly believes that conversion to Christianity will solve the problem of the hydrogen bomb because really redeemed men will not drop the bomb.

"What is disturbing is that organized Protestantism should give its official endorsement to this simple approach to the Christian faith amid the tragedies of the nuclear age and should believe that a great metropolis with all its intricate problems of communal justice will be 'challenged' by Billy's message and that the Church which has abdicated its own convictions for the sake of the campaign will somehow grow in stature because of it."

On Sunday night, June 2, the evangelist spoke to seventeen thousand people on the "Second Coming of Christ." "The Bible mentions the second coming of Christ 380 times in the New Testament," he declared. "The Old Testament is full of references to the return of the Messiah, Christ, and the Anointed One. There can be no permanent peace until he comes. No man today can solve the problems of the world . . . most men cannot understand more than a glimmer. But there is salvation! It is promised in the Bible. It won't be forced on you. Salvation is yours for the taking, only you must reach out and take it."

Early in June, New Yorkers heard news of the first extension. The Garden City *Newsday* reported it thus:

"Billy Graham announced last night that his New York Crusade had been so successful that it will be extended through July 21, three weeks beyond the original closing date. The jubilant evangelist also told an enthusiastic crowd that he plans to preach his July 20 sermon in Yankee Stadium . . . Committee Chairman Roger Hull said last night that the extension will cost at least $55,000 a week and could run total expenses for the crusade to more than $1,000,000."

Next, a fast trip to Philadelphia to the fiftieth American Baptist Convention. "Pray for the sinners in New York and the success of our crusade there," he begged 12,000 ministers.

Three days later, he reviewed the gigantic annual Sunday School Parade of Brooklyn. Over 100,000 youthful marchers from 450 Protestant churches formed 27 separate parades to celebrate the hundred and twenty-eighth anniversary of the founding of the Sunday School Union of Brooklyn. Earlier, before a luncheon group that included Mayor Robert Wagner and Borough President John Cashmore, he spoke at the Montauk Club.

After scouting around the borough behind police escorts, trying to view all twenty-seven parades, he returned to the Garden to report, "What a wonderful thing it is for Christians to get together like that. In the Old Testament, God ordained special religious festivals and feasts, and even today there seems to be a real need for something like that. It's beyond anything I've ever seen. I wish it could be done all over America."

A unique event, the only one of its sort, broke the even pattern of crusade services early in July. The *World-Telegram and Sun* reported it:

"Billy Graham said solemnly last night that the need for a true spiritual revival of America was so urgent that he would be willing to give his life for such a cause. The 38-year-old evangelist, in what was probably the most emotional sermon he has preached, said a great cloud of moral deterioration has descended upon America.

" 'I am tired, weary and worn. The pressures of this crusade have been unbelievably difficult. But I am willing to give my life, ready to die in New York, to see a true spiritual revival in New York and America.'

"Mr. Graham's pledge seemed to affect his audience profoundly. The service took on the aspect of an old-time revival meeting. He asked those willing to dedicate themselves to his crusade's success and 'a regeneration of religious feeling in America' to stand up and pray silently with him. Nearly everyone stood up."

On the afternoon of June 5, police received word that a bomb had been planted in the Garden. Twenty-five policemen plus every Garden guard searched from balcony to basement until only a few minutes before the opening hour. Nothing was found.

Two days later the *Times* called attention to an interesting crusade visitor. He was from Winnipeg and he had traveled three days by bus. The newspaper said, "He dreamed about Billy Graham before the meetings began in New York. In the dream, he saw himself in the Garden moved by the evangelist's call. 'Family tried to talk me out of it,' he related, 'but with that dream I felt I had to go, and I did.'"

How does one keep from saying the wrong thing before a TV camera, Graham had often wondered. In June he appeared on the TV program, "Meet the Press." Afterward, he wrote:

"I sometimes feel extremely nervous before the press and tonight was no exception. I am always afraid of saying something out of place that would bring reproach to Christ and hurt the ministry that He has entrusted to us. I prayed a great deal about this 'Meet the Press' appearance. I believe the Lord helped me to give proper answers. However, after the program, I thought of a great deal more I wish I had said. I also feel that perhaps the men were a little reluctant to push some questions due to the fact that religion is always a bit touchy for men of that caliber. They don't know exactly how to handle it. Sometimes it's a bit amusing to me to watch a newspaper man struggling to understand the complexities and simplicities of religious experience. I always try to use an occasion like this to witness for Christ.

"Went over to Madison Square Garden. Ate a banana and an orange. We were to be on the Steve Allen Show again; that is, the cameras of NBC would pick up six minutes from the Garden at eight-ten. Miss Irene Hicks, who was converted three years ago in our London Crusade, gave a testimony that thrilled everyone; about how she found Christ at Harringay in London and how Christ had kept her ever since. Many people ask the question: Do these converts last? They should hear her testimony. We could bring hundreds to the microphone that we personally know about, and there would be other thousands that we do not know who could come and testify that Christ transformed them and that they have since grown in Him.

"I somehow felt that I missed it on the Steve Allen Show. Nevertheless I am sure it has done some good in reaching a great many people that normally do not go to church. Steve always asks excellent questions."

Readers of New York newspapers enjoyed no such spirited shellackings as were given to Graham during the early part of his 1954 London Crusade. Perhaps the closest thing to a verbal donnybrook was the charge of the Reverend Charles Howard

Graf, rector of the Protestant Episcopal Church of St. John's in the Village.

A United Press story in the Newark *Star Ledger* reported:

"A minister charged from the pulpit of a three-fourths empty Greenwich Village church today that Evangelist Billy Graham is using Madison Ave. advertising techniques to fill Madison Square Garden every night.

"He compared Graham's brand of evangelism with a 'circus' and likened his crowd appeal to that of rock 'n' roll Singer Elvis Presley. The Rev. Charles Howard Graf, rector of St. John's in the Village, said Graham had used 'drum beaters' and a 'sawdust trail' technique to whip interest in his New York crusade.

"Graf based his sermon on the line 'I come to the garden alone,' from the famous hymn 'In the Garden.' He said Graham comes to Madison Square Garden alone every night because the Holy Ghost is not with him.

"'I believe that the Holy Ghost would hesitate to come to Madison Square Garden these days as He would have during that other circus that was there a few weeks ago,' Graf said.

"He referred to the Ringling Brothers, Barnum & Bailey Circus, which ended its annual stand in Madison Square Garden just before Graham moved in."

Only rarely was there an opportunity to escape the web of circumstances that enmesh all who stand in the limelight. This day he saw for himself the way things really were in Harlem and the Bronx. He wrote of one such trip on June 11, and was the better minister for his journey.

"Took a tour of New York this morning with Dan Potter and Mel Ruoss of the Protestant Council. We went all through the Bronx and Harlem, spending about four hours being briefed on the sociological and spiritual conditions of these areas.

"The spiritual and social needs of this city are so staggering that I could not take it all in.

"Three million people come in and out of Manhattan every day. This means that a city as large as Los Angeles is moving out of Manhattan and into Manhattan every single day. We saw areas of fifty and a hundred thousand people where not one single Protestant church exists. We saw one small Episcopal church that was packed and jammed on Sunday, but the minister said that they could only reach out about two blocks in each direction to minister. There are three thousand and four thousand people living on a block—as many as live in the whole of Black Mountain, the little town near my home.

"It is apparent that the Protestant churches of New York are having to face changing conditions. Population shifts are tremendous. A church that seems to be in a good prosperous area one year might be in a totally different type of area within ten years. Church boards are having emergency meetings to decide what to do, whether to close the church or try to adapt to the changing situation. Mel feels that the church does not have contact with the people around it and that the church is not enough of a witness within the social structure. I am inclined to agree with him. However, I feel that the main thrust of evangelism is to get men converted and then send them back as witnesses. The problem in this city is that when people are converted, where are they going to go? There are so many areas in which there is not a Protestant church near them. So many of the Protestant churches are dead and cold—they would offer very little spiritual life to some new convert that has had a wonderful experience with Christ. So the problem is baffling to church leaders. I became convinced that even though we are having great crowds and thousands are finding Christ, yet we are not even scratching the surface of this mighty city."

Another valuable visit was his midnight foray to the shabbiest of Manhattan's communities, the Bowery.

"The gaunt faces, the shambling steps, the bleary eyes, the bitterness and vanished hope.

"Billy Graham saw it all, and he shook his head pityingly," says an AP dispatch.

" 'All of them—so lost in sickness, desperation and ruin.'

"That was his comment last night, after a visit to New York's street of forgotten men.

"He told the audience at his Madison Square Garden Crusade that he and associates spent an hour and a half last night on a lower Manhattan street, with its flophouses and cheap bars, its mumbling, staggering alcoholics with their discolored, puffy flesh and haunted looks.

" 'I believe,' he said, 'that if Jesus were here today He would be down there much of the time with these people who need Him so greatly.' "

A fresh warning reached Catholics—who were reported to be attending in considerable numbers—during the third week in June. The *Journal-American* reported: "A second warning to Roman Catholics against attending evangelist Billy Graham's Crusade . . . It came from the Rev. Richard Ginder, editor of *Our Sunday Visitor,* a national Catholic weekly, which said that tolerance of Graham exists 'only at the social and civil level.'"

Associated Press writer George Cornell said, "The warning—the second in seven weeks—came from Rev. Richard Ginder, editor of *Our Sunday Visitor,* a national Catholic weekly.

"Father Ginder said some Catholics had mistakenly taken the view that their church had given Graham's preaching 'a mild sort of approval.'"

"To correct such assumptions, he is publishing an editorial on the subject in next Sunday's issue of the church publication saying:

"'We are tolerant and friendly to Billy Graham and company just as we are to the Lutherans, Presbyterians and Jehovah's Witnesses.

"'However, our tolerance and friendliness exist only at the social and civil level. It stops dead where religion enters in.'

"The first warning to Catholics about attending Graham's services was sounded in Washington on April 24 by Rev. John E. Kelly, director of the bureau of information of the National Catholic Welfare Conference.

"He described Graham as a purveyor of false doctrines whose teachings were 'a danger to the faith.'"

Crusade boosters got a lift from stories in both the *Times* and the *Herald Tribune* for June 14. The *Times* said, "Forty-four percent of those who made 'decisions for Christ' in the first four weeks of the Billy Graham Crusade here did not have a church affiliation, the Protestant Council of the City of New York reported yesterday . . . the Rev. Dr. Phillips P. Elliott, president of the Council, said that virtually all of those without affiliation were presenting themselves for church membership."

So a partial answer to the conclusions of the *Life* essay began to reach the metropolitan public.

Mondays were supposed to be days of rest. One of Graham's Mondays was reported in *Newsday* under the heading: "Billy Graham, on Long Island Patio, Preaches to 150 Socialites."

"Billy Graham . . . took a holiday yesterday and ended up preaching to a U. S. Supreme Court Judge and 150 socialites on the patio of a fabulous Gold Coast estate.

"The setting was lush and the audience sat on cushioned chairs with cups of punch at their elbows, but Graham's 'few words' were the same brand of evangelism that has echoed across giant meeting halls in this country and abroad.

"Graham, his attractive wife, and eight of his associates were day-long guests at the rolling estate of Mr. and Mrs. Cornelius Vanderbilt Whitney, Old Post Rd. They enjoyed a swim and dinner before the 150 invited guests, including Supreme Court Justice and Mrs. Stanley Reed, started arriving for an intimate meeting and close look at today's most famous evangelist.

"Among the guests were Count and Countess Eugene de Rothschild, Mr. and Mrs. James H. Van Alen, Mrs. Archibald Roosevelt, Mr. and Mrs. C. Champe Taliaferro, Mr. and Mrs. Howard C. Brokaw, Mrs. Thomas Hitchcock, Mr. and Mrs. Alastair B. Martin and Mrs. George Whitney.

" 'The greatest stumbling block to the kingdom of Christ is pride —ego,' Graham told the fashionably dressed audience on the patio overlooking the beautifully manicured gardens of the estate. 'The "I" has to be crucified, the ego denied,' he said. Graham said he knows that some persons who come forward to accept Christ at his meetings are not sincere and do not stay converted, but a good many are. These latter, he said, get to experience 'the sweeping, wonderful, radical change that transforms the whole direction of their lives.' "

Sunday, June 23, was a red-letter day. A giant of a Protestant clergyman, Dr. Daniel A. Poling, editor of the respected *Christian Herald,* came to the pulpit of Marble Collegiate Church, and, with fire in eyes and words, defended Graham and his methods.

He said, "Criticism of the Billy Graham Crusade from within the Protestant faith 'disregards both the facts and rules of fair play.

"The stature of the evangelist is increased as he has refused to answer these critics.

"The records indicate that in great numbers the converts do stand fast.

"Finally, this church and her pastor [Dr. Peale] and the one who speaks this morning, support the Billy Graham Crusade because already this man and his associates in the united effort they have organized with prayer and consecrated service around the world have produced results that honest criticism can neither deride nor ignore."

The evangelist and his team went next to Harlem to conduct an outdoor rally. The rains came and washed away all but five thousand faithful.

Seven days later in July, at the Mall in Central Park, he addressed nine thousand persons of whom approximately seven hundred accepted his invitation.

Three days later he stood on historic ground, the spot where George Washington took his oath as President of the United States, steps of the U. S. Treasury Building on Wall Street, and preached to thirty thousand souls.

"The Founding Fathers believed they had created a nation under God," he said. "What America needs is not more nuclear weapons . . . but more devout Christians."

Three days later he held a meeting for New York's tremendous Spanish-speaking population. Two hundred Spanish churches brought their congregations to Madison Square Garden on Saturday afternoon, July 13. Most of them had never been in the Garden before. They made up a rapt audience of fifteen thousand that Graham addressed through an interpreter. As rapidly as he spoke, the Reverend Rogelio Archilla, a minister of the Spanish Evangelical Church in the Bronx, interpreted his message. An all-Spanish choir sang an anthem. George Beverly Shea even sang a solo in Spanish.

Graham's invitation was accepted by almost one thousand persons.

By now, people were talking again of extending the crusade. But could Graham stand it? Reporters looked at him, wondering, and reported to their readers. Said the Bayonne *Times:*

"His voice, as strong in his last scheduled week as it was when he first came to town, carries the conviction of a young man with the answer. Nevertheless, he looks tired. His eyes are even deeper in the shadows of his brows. He has dropped almost 15 pounds. And his appeal which started off in a controlled low key has grown in ten weeks to a crescendo that suggests nervous energy."

Every war has a crucial battle. Every battle has a crucial point when a moment of decision brings victory or defeat. The crucial moment of the New York campaign came on the morning of July 19, when the executive committee met for breakfast with Graham and his team.

Would the crusade end with the morrow's rally in the Yankee Stadium as had been planned?

Would it drive ahead—perhaps to disaster, but perhaps to unprecedented success?

First there were four prayers to God for guidance, including one from the evangelist. Then Roger Hull introduced the various problems involved and called on Graham for his comment.

Graham said that he had felt for "the last three days" that they should go ahead. An extension beyond Yankee Stadium had been looked on by some as anticlimactic. Graham said that he had searched the Bible for anticlimaxes. He stated, "In Acts, I find the Day of Pentecost. There is a climax! But then the disciples were not reluctant to go ahead. Indeed, I find that they stayed in a city until they were chased out. I believe it is right that we should go on too."

Of those assembled, only one executive committee member, who spoke as an individual and not officially, questioned his position. His argument received close attention. At the end the consensus was phrased by Graham himself. "We'll never have this momentum again," he said. "I feel that even if I'm the only person in the Garden, I've got to stay."

Put to a vote, everyone except the single critic was for continuation. He rose, withdrew his objection, and made the decision unanimous.

That night Roger Hull came to the platform and said, "After prayerful consideration, it has been decided to extend the crusade." For a long moment, you could have heard a pin drop. And then the taboo against hand clapping collapsed and the audience burst into an extended round of applause.

Graham said, "In the beginning, I just did not have the faith to believe this could happen. I admit it frankly. It is God's answer to the prayers of millions. We have never held a crusade longer than twelve weeks anywhere. Here in New York we have already passed the attendance record of that longest crusade which was in London. We believe that very soon we will equal or pass the total number of conversions."

So the stage was set for the final phase, the amazing extension which started next day with an unbelievable crowd of more than one hundred thousand at Yankee Stadium, which grew in vigor through the excitement of Teen Week, and which came to a ding-dong climax at the Crossroads of the World on September 1.

On July 30 Graham's diary received a final, hurried entry. Ten days had passed since the triumph at Yankee Stadium, ten days of the smallest crowds in the entire crusade, ten days of criticism from some commentators that the evangelist had "asked for it" by trying to force his luck. Was he worried or frightened during that last "black week" of July? This is what he said in his last entry:

"During the past three weeks, I have had very little time to write in my diary. These have been three full weeks. The attendance has sagged a bit, our lowest crowds being 14,500, but the number of decisions stays about the same.

"Every service during the past three weeks has been charged with the power of the Holy Spirit. All of us can sense a deepening of God's presence. There is a great sense of conviction in the audience each evening and on some evenings people have come forward at the invitation even before I gave it. One evening we had about seventy-five that were already standing in front to receive Christ before I had finished."

So he answered, in his own mind, the challenge of New York in August, the hot midsummer month when New York was supposed to become a haunted city.

But the ultimate answer would be found, not in the size of the crowds or the number of sermons he preached, but the changed lives of human beings.

These were matters about which an astonishing number of New Yorkers were suddenly beginning to talk.

12

To reach more people, they turned the Garden into a studio-sanctuary, where TV hurled God's message at homes by the millions, and hotel rooms and hospitals . . .

"Go ye therefore, and teach all nations!"

The ancient fathers who practiced those injunctions girded their loins and embarked upon frequently hazardous pilgrimages. Tradition teaches us that Peter went to Babylon and Rome, Andrew to Greece, Bartholomew to Armenia, Thomas to India, Matthew to Ethiopia, James to Egypt, Jude to Persia. . . .

Modern technology provides a modern "proclaimer" with seven-league boots. His pilgrimage is electronic.

On the night of June 1 the New York Crusade thrust outward among shrieking kilocycles to span this continent and give Billy Graham the largest audience in the history of man's quest for God.

Describing his first telecast from the Garden, *Time* said:

"The long arms chopped the smokeless air of Manhattan's Madison Square Garden and the bone-rigid forefinger jabbed at the TV screen. 'Right in your living room,' came the muscular Southern voice, 'Right in your bedrooms, right in a bar, you can let Christ come in.' Wearing TV blue but no make-up, Carolina-tanned Billy Graham was bringing down the third-act curtain on the first live U.S. telecast of his New York Crusade . . ."

A national rating organization called Trendex gave him an estimated audience of six or seven million listeners.

"We couldn't reach that many if we preached a whole year in the Garden," Graham marveled.

TV critics divided opinions. *Variety*, the Bible of show business, reviewed the TV service as they would have any commercial production. "As a one-man evangelism show, it was a revelation and a close insight into why audiences respond to this religious phenomenon. As a showman, Graham's hour performance had all the

118

click elements that translated, say, into the pop music area, make a Lawrence Welk tick. As sure fire as the techniques used by Ralph Edwards in going after the 'heart,' so is the Billy Graham pitch for the 'soul.' . . . Few performers, whether on TV, stage or film, have the dynamic qualities of Graham or are as sure of themselves . . . There's no unctuous quality, no sanctimonious persuasion. The voice is strong, never borders on hysteria. . . . Graham's script was a 'natural' for the occasion—the chapter and verse recital of a world in torment, the escape from unreality . . . and the inevitable return to the thematic, 'The soul is restless until it has found its rest in God!' . . . And the program faded off as hundreds stepped forward."

Marie Torre in the *Herald Tribune* wrote, "Billy Graham is off to an impressive start . . . without a $9,000-a-week writer or a glittering array of star guests, Dr. Graham provided the ABC network with its highest rating for the time period."

Syndicated columnist John Crosby said, "Mr. Graham presents a case for God pretty much like an insurance salesman seeing to it that you are thoroughly covered as the only sensible precaution. . . . This is the age in which the worship of security has transcended the worship of God and the Graham brand of evangelism is, heaven knows, gilt-edged. This, I think, is what bothers me about it. Christianity, after all, was originally a very risky business. Security was not what the early Christians were seeking or what they got."

TV editor Al Davies of the Bayonne, N. J., *Times* entered what he called a minority vote: "I was disappointed . . . but if you are going to review a program, you must call it the way you see it. . . . This is not a good TV program. It is too much sermon, not enough color, not enough music, and misses the climax. . . . Billy's pulpit mannerisms, which may hold a Garden audience, fail completely . . . he uses his hands as if they were a windmill so that the person in the living room loses the Gospel message and becomes just a watcher of the hands . . . maybe Billy Graham, this first telecast under his belt, can do better. . . ."

These were honest opinions from men with no axes to grind. All churchmen agreed that the telecast was a daring foray into the future. No one had known what would happen if a simple gospel, framed in the sanctuary of the Garden, were offered to American homes. A Christian benefactor who insisted on anonymity made the first two telecasts possible by guaranteeing one hundred thousand dollars toward their cost.

The initial letters trickled into Graham's association office in Minneapolis. They were touching, but much like those he had received for years from his weekly "Hour of Decision" broadcasts.

From Wildwood, New Jersey . . . "I am a shut-in, age eighty-six, a war veteran under three flags. Tonight, I gave my heart to God and wish to acknowledge to you my gratitude for happiness."

From Buffalo, New York . . . "I am a good church member but found I wasn't a Christian at heart. Your sermons have opened my eyes and my heart."

From Ceres, California . . . "Your program was enjoyed by my patients and my staff. One eighty-four-year-old patient who was reared a spiritualist accepted Christ. Another gentleman was heard hours later praying, and he explained, 'I'm just confessing my sins.' A wealthy lady sat with tears streaming down her cheeks singing 'Just As I Am.'"

From New York . . . "I feel different now. You see I've been quite sick and very depressed. I have even thought of doing away with myself but now that's all changed. You have just given me something wonderful to live for."

But almost immediately a phone call from Minneapolis told Graham, "All at once this mail is pouring in. It's like a dam broke somewhere. We're getting ten thousand letters a day."

So the public had listened . . . and the public had responded. The second telecast went off without a hitch. Office walls in Minneapolis were bulging as fifty extra girls were hired just to open letters. The entire nation seemed to have something urgent to say to Dr. Graham. Some of the most surprising letters were from children.

From Rogersville, Tennessee . . . "I saw your program and while I was watching, the Lord saved me. I went and joined the church the next day. I am eleven years old and will be in the seventh grade."

From Lynchburg, Virginia . . . "I am seven years old. We watch your program every Saturday night. I took Jesus into my heart tonight. My father and mother are Christians."

From Hershey, Pennsylvania . . . "My husband and I are working as house-parents in a school for orphan boys. It was a real thrill for us to have the boys watch your program. We prayed with most of the boys afterwards and we feel that many of them made a true decision for Christ."

From Union Mills, North Carolina . . . "I am ten years old and visiting my aunt here. While you were preaching I felt heavy inside. I still felt that way after the program so my aunt prayed with me and God saved me. I know I am saved because I felt good all over."

From Kasson, Minnesota . . . "I am having my mother write this for me. I am only seven years old and listen to the telecast on Saturday nights. I gave my heart to the Lord tonight. I want you to have my dollar that I have been saving to win more souls for Jesus."

From North Arlington, New Jersey . . . "Please tell me what I can do each day to improve myself as a Christian. I have been reading the Bible every day. *I am ten years old.*"

From Rock Hill, South Carolina . . . "One of our sons, age nine, listened to every word you said and called me to come hear you. Later, at the supper table he announced that he had reached the age of accountability and he knew the difference between right and wrong. The next morning while in church he whispered that he wanted to go forward and become a Christian."

The evangelist had gone home after his June 8 broadcast deeply impressed by the experience of preaching before a "live" congregation and a TV audience at the same time. He was on the threshold of a period of expansion and outthrust, and he must have sensed its imminence as he wrote about that service in his diary.

"The service tonight was to be televised coast-to-coast again. I had a feeling all afternoon, as I prepared my message, that God was going to give me great liberty and power, which I felt I lacked last week. We had already received something like twenty-five or thirty thousand letters. Literally hundreds had said they had been converted while watching the telecast. Scores of ministers had written saying that new people had turned up in their churches on Sunday morning. We had also received something like thirty thousand dollars in contributions. This was all extremely encouraging. I have begun to feel that perhaps we are holding the Madison Square Garden meetings almost entirely so we could have this telecast from Madison Square Garden.

"The building was jammed to capacity. Cliff was in rare form, feeling good. The choir, I think, sang better than I had ever heard. Then the telecast at eight o'clock. In contrast to last week's telecast, everything went smoothly. From the moment I stood up I knew God was with me. There was great liberty and freedom in preaching and when the invitation was given, one of the most remarkable things happened I think I have ever witnessed. Just before I asked the people to come, a beautiful little girl with long hair came and stood so sweetly in front of the platform. Her hands were crossed, her head was down, and I could see her cheeks were wet with tears. I had not told any emotional stories. There was nothing that could have made her weep except her love for Christ. Millions of Americans saw her by television, and I am sure they must have been moved. It almost looked as though someone had planned it that way—that someone was the Holy Spirit. 'A little child shall lead them.' The whole Garden was moved by that precious scene.

"Then hundreds of others began to stream down the aisles. An hour after the telecast the telephone began to ring from all over America. Telegrams began to pour in. One businessman from Chicago called and said that he had his board of directors watching the telecast, and when it was over, he knelt down in front of them unashamedly weeping, giving his heart to Christ. We are beginning to realize that God can work through the medium of television to bring precious souls to Himself. How we thank God for this great opportunity of communicating the Gospel to additional millions. I preached to more people tonight perhaps than Wesley could have reached in many years. The responsibility is overwhelming and staggering."

Two days later the evangelist's thoughts had crystallized into a conviction that was shared apparently by every member of the Crusade Executive Committee. His diary noted:

"Late in the afternoon I met with the Executive Committee for dinner. They had become so enthusiastic about the crusade that they voted to extend the telecast another three weeks at a cost of about $200,000. This telecast is a tremendous ministry that is far beyond the reach of Madison Square Garden. In fact, I think, when the history of this crusade is written, we will say that the telecasts were by far the most important phase of the ministry. We are reaching more people than we could reach in almost a lifetime at Madison Square Garden. I believe literally thousands are coming to know Christ every Saturday night by the means of television."

The Minneapolis office digested cross sections of the mail for team members in New York, offering proof of the remarkable pudding called television.

Surprising—considering that the telecast was on Saturday night —many letters were from teen-agers:

From metropolitan New York . . . "I am just turning thirteen, the most difficult age. But it is best for me because I have found God. Before I was like all teen-agers. I had bad thoughts and liked to strike back. I was already on probation in school about fights. But now I don't have to worry about getting into trouble. I'm a happy girl now, real joy inside me. Pray that I may become stronger in the Lord."

From Cary, North Carolina . . . "Tonight after hearing your service over television I made my decision for Christ. I am seventeen years old and a member of a church but I had never really made a decision for Christ until tonight."

From Levittown, Pennsylvania . . . "I am thirteen years old. I listened to your television program and I gave myself to God. I prayed like you said and I feel that God received me."

Many letters came from people who were mixed up, disillusioned, or in desperate straits. Knowing no boundaries, TV reached alcoholics, sex-ridden men and women, and dejected mortals who would never have come to a public meeting.

From Rochester, Minnesota . . . "I am an engineering student at Iowa State College. I watched the telecast of your New York Crusade last Saturday night. I originally began to watch it mainly out of curiosity but I found that much in your message seemed aimed directly at me, pointing up many of my own personal problems. Put me down as another 'decision for Christ.'"

From Nitro, West Virginia . . . "These past few weeks your

television program has done more for me than I would ever be able to explain. You have taught me the meaning of the Bible and what it means to be a true Christian. I have been mixed up and confused for some time but not any more. I know what I want. I want to live my life for Christ and so does my husband and that is exactly what we are going to do."

From Philadelphia, Pennsylvania . . . "Sometime ago I wrote to you concerning my problems. I received your wonderful letter in return and thank you so much. I have been praying for myself and my husband. My husband says he will try to give up drinking and go to church. We watched your telecast on Saturday evening and it helped me so much. I made my decision for Christ just sitting there in the living room. We all went to church on Sunday."

From Iowa Falls, Iowa . . . "I made the decision for Christ. The TV reception was poor, due to an electrical storm, but Christ reception was wonderful. I am thirty-six and have been trying to get away from alcohol for years. On the fifteenth I turned my problem over to Christ and I have not been bothered since."

From Jupiter, Florida . . . "I have been fortunate enough to watch you on TV for two Saturday nights. Last evening I bowed my head and prayed to God for forgiveness and for strength to carry on each day. Due to my alcoholism, my husband is doing everything in his power to keep us together, both financially and spiritually, and this morning I can say I am a Christian."

From Manhattan . . . "My wife had left me. I tried to get her back but she refused and her father ran me off his place. I met up with a divorced woman and we liked each other enough to paint the town. We got a hotel room together and I flicked on the TV set and ordered drinks. You were talking about me. You were speaking straight at my sin. When you finished, I got up and left that room and that liquor because I know I was doing wrong. I am reading the Bible now and maybe someday the Lord will come into my heart."

Replies to Billy Graham from grateful families seemed to have been written with special vigor and conviction. He had warned many audiences of America's death march toward immorality and divorce, but never had he received so much written evidence of the effect of God's message.

From Rhodhiss, North Carolina . . . "We listen and see your program every week. I have received a blessing from them. My husband and I were thinking of a separation but since your revival we have been drawn closer to each other."

From Albany, New York . . . "Tonight for the first time I know the feeling of being at peace. Over the past months I have been struggling with temptation that has threatened the happiness of my marriage and threatened to separate me from my husband and my children. I have tried to receive Christ while still holding back part of myself and tried to fight temptation without His help, so to speak. But tonight you spoke of the ego—the I in sin and the I in Lucifer—and I realized that alone I can do nothing and alone I am nothing. I received Christ as my Savior and accepted his love with thanksgiving."

From Union, North Carolina . . . "Before your wonderful sermon last Saturday night my husband and I were about to give up. Our marriage was just about on the rocks. We were constantly bickering and quarreling. We had discussed seeing a marriage counselor. During your sermon God spoke to each of us in a wonderful way. Immediately after, we went into our bedroom, got down on our knees, and gave our hearts to our God. Thank God our marriage is saved."

From Levittown, New York . . . "Thank you for the most inspiring hour that I and my wife have ever spent. We have both given ourselves to Christ this evening and here in the quiet of our living room we do truly feel the warmth and presence of Jesus. Thank you, Dr. Graham."

From Elyria, Ohio . . . "During a talk after the program our two children and I decided that as a family we were missing out on one of the most rewarding experiences a family can have . . . that of worshipping together. Therefore, this household has established the family altar and it truly is a blessing to all of us."

From Dallas, Texas . . . "Right in our living room we had the maid kneel in prayer with us to ask God to bless your every work. It was an honor to have you with us. It was an experience we shall not forget."

An observer of this astounding outreach of Graham's mission

cannot but wonder where it all began. In what brain or intelligence did the first spark gleam? Was it the chance mutation of circumstance plus technology, or was it divinely ordained "before we were born and before the world began," as Graham had said of his meeting individuals who came to the Garden.

A reporter's answer is that many experts have wondered how TV might be used in behalf of the Bible's evangelistic mandate. Even Graham had made unsatisfactory experiments. But nothing like the Garden program had been conceived because there had been nothing in experience like the effect of Graham preaching at the Garden.

The radio programs and supporting activities of the Billy Graham Evangelistic Association are handled by the Walter F. Bennett Advertising Agency of Chicago. Walter Bennett and Fred Dienert are its principals. As much as any, they are responsible for the first discussions about "live" telecasts in the Garden.

But even after such discussions, three things were needed.

Graham's wholehearted endorsement.

A suitable and available hour on a network schedule.

And money. About sixty thousand dollars each week.

Of the three, the first was certainly the most significant. It would have been easy for Graham to reject the difficult and untried. In the vernacular, "Graham had a good thing going." His houses were "standing room only." Showmen told him that nothing could kill a personality so fast as TV exposure. Telecasts might possibly write a fast finis to his mass ministry.

He heard the arguments and then prayed his way to a decision. "We'll try it if you can clear the time," he told Bennett and Dienert.

The time was cleared after much effort, a Saturday-night span of sixty minutes offered by the American Broadcasting network.

The money was pledged for the first two Saturdays, and two more were ordered on faith because the TV firm would sell only in four-week segments.

And electronic mass evangelism was born!

From the beginning, his listeners offered support in touching, tender, yearning letters like these:

From Bremerton, Washington . . . "We would like to tell you that we accepted Christ last night. We are sending an offering.

It isn't very much but it is all we have. Maybe it will help some other couple to accept Christ and find the wonderful peace he can give."

From Stowe, Pennsylvania . . . "My husband and I watch television and saw the hundreds come forward and give their hearts to Christ. Enclosed is two dollars for your work."

From Appleton, Wisconsin . . . "My little boy started to save for a new bicycle but after watching you on television, he came to me and said, 'Dad, please send this dollar to Billy Graham.'"

From Greenville, Delaware . . . "My soul feels much better now and I know if I had been at the Garden I would have accepted Christ in person. Here at home I did it just the same and I feel like a great load has been taken off me. Please accept this contribution from a 'new' fifteen-year-old."

So the money came by dribs and drabs until each week, give a little, take a little, there was enough to pay all the bills. There was even enough to make a plan for tomorrow.

All future Graham crusades are expected to follow the pattern set in Madison Square Garden, and each stadium or arena in which the evangelist places his pulpit will become his studio-sanctuary. Already a fund for this purpose has been started by the New York Crusade Executive Committee, thus establishing another channel by which God's people of one community can reach across the nation to help others.

By the crusade's end, one other aspect of the impact of the TV ministry became clear. *It was returning backsliding church members to church.* Equally amazing, pastors were reporting strange faces in their congregations, with many newcomers seeking a church home.

Such as these:

"I am a young man of nineteen and for years have been a church member. A few minutes ago I bowed down in front of my TV, accepted Jesus as my Redeemer. I am a Sunday School teacher and very active in all church work but on the side I have been living a sinful life."

Another . . . "You have done for me in two weeks what my

church had not been able to do in six years. I have been a Christian but after hearing you I want to be a better and stronger one. I want to help others as you have helped me."

From a widow . . . "When you said you don't need to know everything, all you need to know is your need of Jesus, it hit me right between the eyes. It gave me assurance that we trust His word and not the loss of our joy or circumstances. I am a widow with children and the problems are not easy."

From a churchman . . . "A family who heard your first Saturday telecast came to our church on the following Sunday and took the Lord as their Savior."

From a deacon . . . "Our pastor announced that he had requests from three different families after the Saturday program, to come and help them settle them down to find peace with God, because the Holy Spirit had been working in them and they wanted counseling."

From a minister . . . "You will be heartened to know that we have received three persons by confession of faith into our church who made their decisions on Saturday night as they viewed your program."

From an elder . . . "It is thrilling to hear your TV program. It effected our minister, too. He gave his first real altar call in seven years and four people went forward."

From a pastor . . . "The parents of a young man who left a good position to enter the ministry have hated me for it. Tonight I went to their home and the mother was going to see 'what all this fanaticism is about.' We tuned in your program and, when you gave the invitation, she wept like a baby, dropped to her knees and accepted Christ. We're praying for you."

Journalistic caution requires a historian to doubt the sincerity of perhaps a few items of this massive impersonal testimony. No doubt can exist, however, of TV's successful outreach when it is reported time after time by a responsible third party. Space permits only this single example.

It comes from the Reverend Joe L. Robbins, of the Trinity Baptist Church, Wichita, Kansas. He wrote:

"While I was away during my vacation, a family attended our services every Sunday. Then when I returned they immediately invited me to their home to talk about their relationship to God.

"I don't believe I have ever seen a couple more willing to receive Christ. The man could hardly wait until I had read some Scripture and clearly described what is involved in being a Christian. We knelt together in the living room of their home and heaven was there, believe me. They completely surrendered themselves to Christ. After confession of their sins, and receiving Christ, they immediately talked of the church, the purpose of it, what we can do for Christ in belonging to it. In the years of ministry, I never felt a couple so ready to accept the claims of Christ our Lord.

"They first began thinking about their relationship to God while listening to one of your programs over television from the Garden. It had never bothered them until that night. May God bless your great effort and earnestly I believe the revival campaign in New York has left its impact upon all America."

"If but one single soul is saved," Graham said at this crusade's outset, "it would be worth all the money."

13

Slowly the tide began to turn. As Graham's clear charges hit their mark, men would say, "These things any one can understand. I am sorry for my sins. I accept Christ. I will follow God's will."

New York cabbies began to take the crusade seriously about four weeks after Graham's first Garden service. It took them that long to get over the shock of what their fares were telling them.

"This Billy the Kid, what's his angle?" they asked.

"He wants you to be happy. He wants you to have everlasting life."

They tried another tack. "Those big collections every night. He must be making a pile, huh?"

"He doesn't get a penny. Every cent goes toward expenses."

After a while, putting all their answers together, they began to tell their fares about Graham. "As I get it, this guy makes religion like A-B-C," they said. "Besides, he won't claim no credit for himself for these crowds or nothing. He's a guy you don't mind listening to."

It is a known fact that any project that can set Manhattan's cab drivers to talking is assured of success, which applies to Broadway shows, ball teams, and TV programs. It applied, also, perhaps, to the crusade.

One night a visitor told his driver, "You put your cab in that parking lot. I'll pay for it. We'll go in and hear Graham together." It happened dozens of times.

Another night a pugnacious hackman spoke about Graham so acidly that his fare, who happened to be a crusade counselor, answered with a fervent lecture on Christianity. Later, as the counselor stood among the inquirers who had come forward, he noticed a man whose face was vaguely familiar.

"Don't I know you from somewhere?" he asked.

"Could be," the stranger said.

"Maybe we've done business together?"

"We sure have," said the man. "I drove the taxi that brought you here."

Graham had said long ago, "If they talk of me and not about God, then I shall have failed." In New York, during the second month, people began to talk of Billy and God. All of a sudden, religion was less mysterious and more immediate. People became aware that "doing good" was not all that was required of a Christian. Listening to the evangelist, they heard that Jesus Christ was mankind's only intercessor and the only channel through which man could reach God. Watching Graham, they sensed the inward joy of his faith.

"I am glad," he told the thousands who listened, "that I have been adopted in His family . . . not through any good work that Billy Graham has done. Billy Graham deserves hell. Not through any goodness that I've done, not through any righteousness of merit of my own. I am saved tonight. I am a member of the body of Christ tonight only because of what He did at the Cross. The fact that God raised him from the dead and is ever-living to make intercession for us."

Billy Graham's message to New York was the same that he had preached throughout the world. Now he felt he faced a special challenge. "The problem of Manhattan," Billy said, "is that only 7½ per cent of the city is Protestant. London was basically Protestant, and it had a deep religious tradition, but it had gone to sleep. But New York is 93 per cent *antagonistic* to such a crusade as this.

"Most of the people in New York . . . they're not against God; they just don't have time for Him. But I want to tell you this: although you may not care for God, God cares for you! He loves you, knows your troubles and your heart, and offers you deliverance and new life in Jesus Christ."

To persuade the people of New York and the people of the world to care about God, Graham has carefully sought ways to make himself an acceptable, forceful persuader, an instrument by which God's wishes can be not only understood but fulfilled.

Billy Graham has an electric personality. The spark within him glows to such an extent that his passionate enthusiasm communicates itself to his listeners. But he exhorts, not like a Messiah urging his followers, but as a human who enjoys the blessings that receiving Christ has given him, and who is eager to have all mankind embraced into the family of God.

Thus Graham speaks to his audiences as one man to another. He is one of them. The occasional presence of his wife or mother at the crusade supports the belief that he is like the man in the balcony, or in the second row, or in the crowd in the street. He further ties himself to the audience by bringing them into his preaching. He will make a statement and suddenly tack on a fast "Did-you-know-that?" He will say, "Brains cannot answer the moral question, did you know that?" Or, "No man has ever turned away from Christ happy, did you know that?"

Describing a biblical event, he will say, "I want you to see Paul being stoned, beaten, left for dead. . . . I want you to see Paul betrayed, shipwrecked."

Again and again, you! You! YOU!

If he senses that his audience is harboring a doubt about some point, he disarms them by putting their unasked question thus: "But look here, Billy," he will exclaim. "You say I can be a Christian and be popular at the same time," or, "But wait a minute, Billy! You say the Bible explains why so many of those who sin seem to prosper?"

Often he clothes his statements with mystical significance.

"I want you to listen with the ears of your soul as well as your physical ears. While I'm speaking, you will be conscious of another voice, deep down inside. That is the voice of God. Pay careful attention to that voice. Every person present is here by divine appointment. This is no accident, *this meeting was planned before we were born.*"

Graham has always felt that he cannot preach except in a way which will interest the people who come to hear him. Doing so, he feels a certain—almost supernatural—power within him. After a meeting in May he wrote in his diary:

"Tonight I felt probably the greatest liberty I have felt thus far. I doubt if there is an experience in the world quite like a minister preaching the Gospel and having liberty and power. It is beyond any other human experience. There is nothing more horrible than to preach without liberty and power. I have had ministers tell me that they never had liberty or power in preaching. . . . I think I would leave the pulpit."

Some critics accuse Graham of disregarding theological problems, but his concern is just as deep and real as that of most ministers. He feels, however, that he must talk simply to an audience made up largely of unchurched people and folk who are immature theologically.

Thus most of Graham's sermons are frank variations on the theme of being born again. The Bible says, "Verily, verily, I say unto thee, except a man be born again, he cannot see the Kingdom of God." Over and over, he declares, "The Bible says . . ."

His theme argument runs: First, all mankind has sinned. Second, sin separates man from God. Third, as long as man is separated from God he is unhappy and unfulfilled.

His sermons make these points:

God created man in his own image and then permitted him to have his own free choice of sinning or not.

Adam chose his own way. This rebellion was Adam's great sin because it resulted in separation from God.

The sin of Adam is the sin in which mankind has partaken.

Retreating from a round of newspaper interviews, Ruth Graham ironed her husband's shirts. Broadcast equipment for *The Hour of Decision* filled the corner of their hotel room.

Billy Graham took the Gospel to people wherever they would listen. An open-air rally sponsored by the Heart of Harlem Neighborhood Association of the Protestant Council was rained out, but after the heavy storm, a crowd of 5,000 returned to hear the evangelist deliver his message from the steps of the Salem Methodist Church at Seventh Avenue and 129th Street.

Every night, inquirers crowded around Graham's pulpit until there was no more room. Invariably the evangelist stood back, arms folded, almost as if he were stepping aside for the Holy Spirit. Often he said, "It's not Billy Graham calling you. The quicker you forget my name, the better. It's Jesus who is passing by."

We may keep every commandment and live blameless lives but we are still sinners.

Because God so loved mankind, He sent His Son, Jesus, as a bridge by which men could return to God. Jesus did this by dying on the Cross, thereby atoning for and taking onto Himself the sins of all mankind. In his death on the Cross and His resurrection, He became the intercessor before God for each person who would believe in Him as Savior.

In the Garden counseling room, those who made decisions were requested to repeat a prayer of confession:

"I am a sinner.

"I need salvation.

"Jesus died to save me.

"By faith and belief in God's word, I accept Jesus in my heart as my Savior. I turn from my sin. I renounce my sin. From henceforth I will live for Jesus and serve Him."

When a man surrenders to Jesus, Graham explains, the spirit of God, who is the Holy Spirit, fills and suffuses him, body, heart and soul, and guides him henceforth.

Thus a man is "born again" and comes immediately into the family of God.

Graham's mission at Madison Square Garden was to persuade his hearers to take the simple steps that led to being born again. A part of that task was to simplify religious conundrums.

His diary for June 8 reveals one such effort:

"For the rest of the day I prepared my sermon on the Mystery of Conversion. I read a great deal in Strong's *Theology* on the subject of conversion, regeneration, repentance and faith, collecting some new ideas and ways of expressing this subject that I preach on so much. It seems to me that it is difficult to put in chronological order just which comes first, repentance, faith, or regeneration. It's like saying: which comes first, the chicken or the egg? They all seem to happen simultaneously. It is also rather difficult to understand the difference between the sovereign, irresistible Grace of God and man's free will.

"It seems to me that both are involved. When I preach, I am certain that I am preaching to people whom God has chosen and yet that is not my problem: I am to preach directly to their wills. I remember something Spurgeon said: 'I know that all those that God has chosen are going to be saved tonight, and if one of you

133

comes whom God has not chosen, I believe He will receive you.'"

More than any man in his generation, Graham has tried to make God meaningful in every area of life. His God inhabits churches but He also fills woods, fields, and the stratosphere. He says that Christ can enter your heart no matter where you are. Thousands from his TV audience wrote exuberantly that they had fallen on their knees in their homes and made a decision.

Some viewers are critical, of course. One lady considered it probable that he could improve his sermons if he sat in the quiet of a New York park disguised in workman's clothes. Another, a college professor, corrected his pronunciation. A third insisted that America was damned because the U.S.A. had defied God by building the Panama Canal despite the Bible warning that "What therefore God has joined together, let no man put asunder."

Trying to put his message into simple phrases, Graham often grew tired through the long days of sermon after sermon, but always something guided him.

"Preached on the Great Judgment Day," he wrote. "Was too weary to put much energy into the sermon, yet I could sense the Holy Spirit speaking through me and could sense probably greater power than any service yet. When the invitation was given, they started coming forward before I was finished. I do not know how many came forward, but I believe tonight was one of the largest of the crusade. To God be the glory!"

Another entry: "Preached on the Prodigal Son. Felt somewhat bound, not as much liberty as normal. The crowd was about the same as the night before. It was very hot and humid. I think we had about the smallest response to the invitation we have had yet. I seem to sense that there is a greater response to the invitation when I preach on judgment than any other subject. Tonight I preached more on the love, mercy, and grace of God, and the response is not nearly so great. Perhaps the message for New York is judgment."

In the vast range of his sermons—from sex to the end of the world—he never hesitated to use topics which might "scare people to Christ," although they were a minor thread in the whole tapestry.

One night he told of his general dislike of the subject of hell, but he said, "I must preach it because Jesus said so much about it, and because it is an act of mercy to warn men when they face anything so terrible. Hell was never prepared for man; it was prepared for the Devil. But if you persist in following the Devil, the Bible says you will spend eternity where he will—in hell."

He constantly urged his listeners to give themselves to Christ before it was too late. One man, he said, came to the Garden and felt God speaking, but resisted. He gritted his teeth and refused to give up his pride and yield his life. He went home, sat down to drink a glass of milk, and never got up. He was dead of a heart attack. "That man had turned down Christ for the last time," Billy warned. "You never know when your last chance comes, and so I ask you to listen very carefully tonight."

Graham knows that intellectuals pooh-pooh fear as a motive for accepting Christ. "I teach my children up on the mountain where we live to beware of rattlesnakes, lest they be bitten and die. This is a legitimate fear." Fear of God, fear of judgment, he believes, is a legitimate fear.

Of love he has much to say. First of all, it must be love of God, the Creator.

Are there any other gods that Americans worship? Yes! says Billy. "New York has a thousand gods. Some think God is a sour-faced cosmic policeman; some think God is a heavenly grandfather with a Santa Claus beard. For many people, fame is god, and they have sold their souls to achieve notoriety. Millions worship money and will put God and family and everything else behind them to make another five dollars. There are men who have determined to get to the top of their company, and their friends and their honor have been sacrificed. Entertainment and pleasure are gods for many! But you must make a choice."

He says that many make a god of their ego and illustrates it deftly:

"Spell the word, sin. S-I-N. The 'I' is in the middle.

"Spell the word, pride. P-R-I-D-E. The 'I' is in the middle.

"Spell the Devil's right name, Lucifer. L-U-C-I-F-E-R! Again, the 'I' is in the middle. And the Devil is in pride and in sin. I! I! I! Your 'I' is your sin. God comes first."

A memorable part of every Graham sermon was the final moment when he extended God's invitation to repent. In a slow, muted voice usually, he began. . . .

"I am going to ask you to come. Up there—down here—I want

you to come. You come—right now—quickly. I am going to ask you to get up out of your seats from all over the place—quietly and reverently—and come and stand here for a moment. Say, 'To-night I receive Christ. I give my life to Christ. I will serve and follow Him from this moment on.' If you are with friends or relatives, they will wait for you."

"Don't let distance keep you from Christ. . . . It's a long way, but Christ went all the way to the Cross because He loved you. Certainly you can come these few steps and give your life to Him. It's an act of your will. You come right now! I am going to ask that every head is bowed right now, in prayer." Softly the choir began to sing, "Just As I Am."

"Men, women, young people, get up out of your seats and come. Stand quietly here tonight and say, 'I give myself to Christ.' Come right now while the choir sings. Christians, you pray!"

Sometimes Graham prayed silently and then added one more plea:

"The decision is up to you. No one can make it for you. I remember when I sat there in that tabernacle in Charlotte, North Carolina. They were singing the last verse of the song when I went forward. That first step was the hardest I ever took in my life. But when I took it, God did the rest. I woke up the next morning, and I *knew* I had been changed. *You* can make a decision tonight that will change your life. You can be born again and you'll never be the same!"

14 *And special rewards came to those who helped, the volunteer soldiers of God's Army, and particularly to those who sang in the choir.*

One night in June an ample, handsome, gray-haired Negro lady walked stiffly to the microphones banked across Graham's pulpit. Organ and grand piano sent a quavering chord into the balconies, and suddenly a famous voice leaped through loud-speakers into nineteen thousand hearts. The song was "Nobody Knows the

Trouble I've Seen." On other nights, spaced through the whole crusade, because she missed only one of all those ninety-seven Garden meetings, she sang "Just a Closer Walk With Thee," and "His Eye Is on the Sparrow."

With the muted choir behind her, with the yearning and artistry of her race in every syllable, she turned each stanza into a holy moment of surpassing beauty. She was Ethel Waters, whose life itself is a sermon. To have grossed a million dollars as one of Broadway's most dazzling singing stars and to be "broke at fifty-six, heavily in debt to the U. S. Government for back taxes, and generally insecure, is an embittering fate," says *Ebony* magazine. Listening to her, nobody could have guessed it.

She sang at first like all the others of those five thousand volunteers, accepting Cliff Barrows' invitation through their churches, rehearsing, and adding her voice to the many in simple anonymity. Weeks passed before Cliff Barrows led her to a mike.

"I just thank the Lord," she said, "that he has spared me long enough to take part in this crusade. When I heard about it, I knew I had to be in it. When I came, it was more than I had dreamed. I feel that through Billy Graham, the Master has given this sinful city of New York a reprieve. Before his coming, few Christians had the guts to praise openly their love and faith or belief in our Lord. But now our Father, through Billy, has broken through the barrier and we use the words 'Jesus Christ' with reverence and humility instead of profanely and blasphemously."

Others, not as famous, also were deeply moved by their participation in the choir. Sitting two thousand strong behind Graham, they became part of a unique corps. While their voices lent inspiration to others, within themselves they discovered room for spiritual excitement that was previously unsuspected.

A Puerto Rican soprano said, "I finally have the feeling, for the first time in my life, of being a Christian. No matter what denomination or race, I now know we are all for the same God."

A young tenor rejoiced, "I really have a zest for living. I know I am going in the right direction. My sins and inferiority complex no longer weigh me down and control me."

A Baptist soprano from Brooklyn said, "God and I have drawn closer to each other. It isn't just singing but 'living' the hymns I sing."

A young teen-ager who sang almost nightly in the bass section wrote to Graham of his almost miraculous transformation.

"I was born and raised in a Christian home, and baptized and confirmed in the Methodist Church. In spite of all this my life began to sink lower and lower. I began early to swear and tell dirty stories. I began to smoke and then to drink . . . My mother (God bless her) brought me to the Garden on May 29. Everything had gone wrong that day and I was in a terrible mood. When Mr. Graham gave the invitation to come forward and accept Christ, a tremendous battle raged in my soul. On the last verse of "Almost Persuaded," I saw a boy younger than myself going forward. At that moment I felt as though I would explode, and I got up and came forward.

"I gave my life to Christ and overnight I stopped drinking, smoking and swearing. Now I am a Christian. Since then, not a day goes by when I don't read the Bible, sing some hymns and pray. As I am only sixteen, I have considered making the ministry my life work. I am going back to Sunday school, where I will talk to people my own age about what God has done for me."

Gradually people all over New York began to hear that many of those attending the crusade were leading changed lives. The same thing was happening among all kinds of volunteers but especially, so it seemed in the early days, among those who sang.

Its members had joined for many reasons. One man and wife, explaining their presence, said, "We came to the Garden and were so inspired by the music that we just had to become a part of it so we could help inspire others."

A young man refused to join with his own church group until he attended his first Garden service. "Then I made my decision and joined up so I could contribute my part to the crusade."

One New Yorker, in search of a seat, got in the choir by mistake, and promptly became a permanent member.

Some choristers came from choirs as far away as Florida, volunteering by mail, and then driving one thousand hot and dusty miles.

A singer told of gaining a new recruit in the subway.

"My friends and I were going home when a young man struck up a conversation one night. We told him we'd been to the crusade and he seemed interested. He moved closer and we could smell whiskey on his breath. 'Tell me about this so-called Billy Graham,' he said.

"We said, 'Why don't you come and see for yourself? Jesus loves you. Hearing Dr. Graham would be good for your soul.'

"'Not for me,' he said. 'My soul's already rotted. Nothing can help it.'

"Well, that was three weeks ago. I'd given up hope that he would ever come, but tonight I was looking around, and behold! There he sat in the front row of the bass section. Yes, he had already given his life to Christ."

Many members made real sacrifices.

A practicing physician gave up night calls and drove 125 miles a day to reach the Garden. Proudly he said, "I welcome this opportunity to witness to others."

A soprano from New Jersey collapsed from physical exhaustion twice during the crusade. In addition to choir work, she and her husband were counselors, and he served as an usher. "We would not have it otherwise for this fruit-bearing season of salvation," she said. "A feeling of shame comes over me even to mention the infinitesimal cost to us."

A Puerto Rican member had to work nights, but "with the help of God, I have managed to work *before* and *after* the meetings."

Another singer said, "As a night nurse I have dedicated one half a day's sleep daily to work in the crusade."

They came because they *wanted* to be in the Garden. Some— only a handful, to be sure—attended every single night. "If Billy Graham can stand up to it, so can we," they declared.

One proud group had a perfect attendance record, a mother-soprano, daughter-alto, son-tenor, and father-bass.

A young married couple, on their way home after a service, noticed a woman sitting in the park who was so obviously in difficulty that they stopped. She told them tearfully that she had taken her two boys and fled from her home, where her drunken, blasphemous husband had made life intolerable. Now she was searching her soul and trying to gather strength to face the future.

"We can't help you, but God can," they told her. "We'd like to pray for you, if you don't mind."

In the park, all three knelt together.

Next day, on their advice, she visited the Garden and met a counselor. Again there were prayers, and these led to the mother placing her whole trust in God, and then she went forth with confidence to rebuild the lives of her sons and herself.

Graham said over and over, "I believe we stand on the threshold of a revival that may sweep all America." If it comes, the ministry of music of Cliff Barrows—no one ever called him by his proper title, which is "the Reverend Clifford Barrows"—will have done more than its share to ignite the flame.

Within the Garden the choir gave each service its special beauty, but beyond the walls, as choristers dispersed to boroughs and suburbs, there were many services over and above the call of words and music. One young lady exulted, "I am born again! It is a joy to last me all my life. The crusade has given me a slight taste of what heaven will be when we are all around the throne of God singing songs of adoration, glory, and thanksgiving."

And that—perhaps—is the beginning of revival.

15 *While the corps of counselors did the work for which they had trained, they found their own lives blessed . . .*

The Wykoff Baptist Church of Wykoff, New Jersey, is a remarkably sturdy, young fellowship. Two years ago, it bought ten acres of residential property holding a thirteen-room house, a garage large enough to hold three cars, and a goat barn. Under its pastor, Larry McGuill, the buildings were converted to religious purposes.

The home became a chapel. The barn became a children's church. The garage became a hotrod club.

This church, like all the other Protestant churches in the Greater New York area, received a letter one day describing the Billy Graham Crusade, its method of operation, and the need, among other things, for approximately four thousand volunteer counselors.

The pastor, as requested, submitted the names of several of his members as candidates for the counselor training course. It was a simple act of faith and co-operation. He took the letter writer's word that experience as a counselor would be a blessing.

Months later, he had one brief glance into an experience that left him humbled and grateful for his role. The *Moody Monthly* magazine tells the story:

"Pastor McGuill remembers walking toward the prayer room with the crowd of inquirers. He heard someone at his side say, 'My hands are wet with perspiration and I'm shaking inside. I've never pointed anyone to Christ before.' He turned to see who it was. It was one of his own members, a mother of two small children. He said to her, 'Elsa, you pray for me, and I'll pray for you, and I know the Lord will help both of us.'

"On the way home on the bus, he noticed that Elsa kept looking out the window without saying a word. Taking a seat beside her, he asked her how she made out.

"Misty-eyed, she answered, 'It was wonderful. My counselee was an older woman. She had spent several years in a Nazi concentration camp in Germany and saw her husband murdered. She came out hating God, and was very bitter. She went to the Garden mostly out of curiosity, and the Lord spoke to her. Pastor, I'm so happy—I led her to the Lord!'

"Summing it all up, Pastor McGuill concluded, 'I'm thrilled at the wonderful results that are happening nightly at the Garden but I am even more thrilled at what is happening in my own little church.'"

If the crusade could be said to have had an elite corps, surely its counselors qualified. They were hand picked. They were specially trained at ninety-minute sessions each week for nine weeks. Ten convenient training locations were set up that covered every one of each of ten metropolitan areas.

In the beginning, some among those invited had mental reservations. They did not trust Graham's theology. They did not like the idea of mass evangelism.

One layman said so to an instructor. "But the counselor turns mass evangelism into personal evangelism," the teacher said. "When an inquirer meets Christ, it is not part of an emotion-struck crowd. He is sitting next to a Christian, a friend, a counselor who has an open Bible and the training to discuss any ordinary problem. If the counselor finds himself in deep water, he summons a spiritual adviser who is usually a minister or layman long experienced in personal work."

A tough-minded layman was undecided about accepting the bid to be a counselor. Gloomy doubts about Graham's theology filled his thoughts. After prayer and meditation, he enrolled. Following the third class, he announced, "This has been a time of wonderful inward growth. All the doubts are now erased from my mind."

A New Jersey schoolteacher, educated in her state's university and teacher's college, eagerly accepted. In mid-course, she said, "I have studied under many instructors, but no course ever satisfied me as much as this one."

A beautiful young actress who was a member of a Hollywood church enrolled. She was in New York to study under the best drama teachers, but something impelled her to take the Bible lessons. After two sessions she made the discovery that she did not know the road to salvation herself.

"I'm quitting," she told her instructor. "I'm not qualified to counsel anybody."

Persuaded to finish the course, she finally sought out a minister and confessed that she was not a Christian. But she was among those who hurried forward to confess when Graham extended his first invitation. Thereafter, she became one of the most faithful of counselors.

Lest it be thought that the nine classes for counselors made up a snap course, every church member is invited to test his own knowledge of Scripture with these questions:

What is the heart of the Gospel message?

Why do all men have need of the application of this message?

What does the Bible declare to be the penalty for sin?

What does the Bible say concerning our ability to merit salvation?

Explain briefly how one becomes a child of God.

How can one know for certain that one has eternal life?

Counselors were expected to read and remember the Scriptural answers to a host of excuses, for example:

I don't believe the Bible! (John 7:17; I Cor. 2:14)

There is too much to give up! (Matthew 6:33; Mark 8:36–37)

I could never keep it up! (I Peter 1:5; Philippians 1:6)

I would rather not do it now! (II Corinthians 6:2; Hebrews 2:3)

Instructions, both verbal and printed, insisted upon an attitude of understanding and patience. Some critics have assumed that a counselor is a sort of grand inquisitor who wrings confessions from unwilling victims.

Here are some of their instructions:

Do not push for a decision. Let him wait if he is not ready now. If the inquirer is in a hurry, do not detain him unnecessarily.

If you feel led to speak to someone in the audience (during the invitation), do so quietly. But DO NOT PRESS FOR A RESPONSE.

This spirit carried through the Counselor Bulletins that went out regularly to repair errors of omission or commission. Bulletin No. 5 carried this interesting admonition:

"It has come to our attention that several counselors have suggested that inquirers go to their church. It has also been brought to our attention that some counselors are openly condemning the present church with which the inquirer is affiliated. REMEMBER THE INSTRUCTIONS GIVEN IN THE COUNSELING CLASSES. DO NOT PROSELYTE OR CONDEMN. The counselors' job is to do all that is possible to make sure the inquirer is rightly related to Jesus Christ."

Two rows of seats across the front of the Garden's main floor were reserved for counselors, six hundred each evening. Their duties began when Graham gave the invitation and converts started forward.

Now it was their job to pair themselves with inquirers, either on their own or as designated by team members before the platform. The pairing theory holds that a male inquirer is more likely to talk to another male, that a young inquirer will readily unburden himself to another teen-ager, and so on. The ideal arrangement would be for people of similar age, sex, background, and interests to meet. This is obviously impossible.

Nevertheless, it happened with a frequency that mystified newsmen. One night, a well-dressed middle-aged counselor led a well-dressed, middle-aged inquirer into the counseling room. Giving his name, he added, "I'm a Lutheran and I live in Cleveland, Ohio."

The astonished inquirer said, "I hope you'll believe me when I tell you that I'm a Lutheran too! And I'm from Cleveland! God must have directed you to me."

A Puerto Rican convert was telling about himself. "By profession, I'm a concert pianist," he said. The counselor said, in amazement, "I, too, am a concert pianist."

A science teacher was assigned to counsel a young man. The inquirer had grave doubts about the Bible and he wanted to resolve them before he commenced his studies to become a science teacher.

A counselor who heads a Norwegian import business was paired with an inquirer who, it developed, also ran a Norwegian import business.

A builder and contractor from Long Island was assigned a man of his own age and general character. "What do you do, sir?" he asked. The inquirer replied, "I'm a builder of small homes in New Jersey."

So many had adventures. A counselor said, "On the second night of my counseling, an inquirer refused to give me her name, which I needed to fill out her decision card. I wondered, what shall I do? Shall I let her go or call an adviser? As the Reverend Blinco spoke, I prayed that God would fill my mouth with the right words. Presently, when I talked, my inquirer began to listen. After prayer together, she gave her name, put her arms around me, kissed me, and thanked me. How wonderfully God saw my need. I don't know when I felt his power so keenly and quickly."

One night a motherly-looking woman approached a counselor and said, "How do I become a Christian? I have a very difficult problem."

The counselor gave her the biblical answers and said, "I would like to pray for you." At the close of his prayer, he asked the woman to pray. In faltering words she said, "Lord forgive me of my sins. Give me peace. Help me solve my problems." She began to weep and between sobs the counselor heard her say, "My son . . . my son . . ."

"Is your son in difficulty?" he asked.

The woman said, "He's one of the boys in the teen-age gang that killed that polio victim." Sobbing, she confessed that he had first got into trouble because of her home situation. She had left his father, remarried against the boy's wishes, and he had turned to his neighborhood gang for security and friendship.

Now in police custody he refused even to see her.

"How can I face the future?" she demanded.

144

"Place your problems in the hands of Christ," the counselor said. "If you confess your sins and ask for guidance, he will give you whatever strength you need."

Several counselors were asked: Has the crusade changed your life in any way?

Their answers:

"I have always been timid about talking to others. Now I know what to say and God has given me the courage to say it."

"It has given me wisdom in dealing with all types of people."

"I am more sensitive to the needs of others."

"I have become stronger through patience and faith."

"My friends know the difference. I have surrendered all."

"For the first time in my life, I feel wanted and needed."

"It has made me more aware of my blessings and made me want to share those blessings with others."

A grateful mother who spent dozens of nights at the Garden named enough blessings to fill a horn of plenty.

"My husband went forward, a wonderful answer to prayer," she said.

"Two of my children sang in the choir and grew spiritually.

"My other two sons attended many meetings and we were all drawn closer together.

"My daughter became engaged to a young man she met in the choir.

"But most of all, it has been thrilling to hear the name of Jesus exalted night after night, and hearing the hundreds of converts confessing the Lord Jesus as their Savior."

Stories such as these do not make newspaper headlines. Their place is in the gossip of women in supermarkets and the talk of men in commuter coaches. So the headline readers could only assert, "Graham is dead. I haven't seen a story on him for a month." The faces of the people who left the Garden counseling room each night told another tale.

They told that the helpers themselves were being helped. These thousands of elite counselors were walking into each night with eyes aglow and heads held high. This did not surprise Graham or his team, but it was something new to the average Joe living in a Manhattan walk-up or suburban split-level. And so they talked about it, about the people they knew who were suddenly talking about Jesus Christ, as if he were a wonderful guy who

145

lived right upstairs and would come down and baby sit if called on.

This was the ground swell of excitement that began to roll through the crowded acres of the giant metropolis.

16 *Now teen-agers came to listen, and parents, too, and many walked forward hand in hand to make decisions during the memorable nights of Teen Week at the Garden . . .*

The Garden audience listened raptly to the young speaker standing in Billy Graham's pulpit. Cliff Barrows had said his name was Zeke, a juvenile delinquent with a police record of eighteen offenses. He looked like what he was. He talked like what he was.

Licking his lips and twisting his fingers, he said:

"I don't know where to start except where it all began. Things were pretty bad. I didn't care about anybody. Somebody would come up and talk—I'd just as well hit him with a pipe.

"Last summer a guy come to our neighborhood. He kinda tricked us into it. He said, did we want to go out to a dude ranch. We wondered what this guy wanted from us. Who was he? He'll take us away for nothin'? That never happened before. Then we heard about those girls who were gonna be out there. We made up our minds we'd go.

"We got there and things were a little different, people were strange. We said, 'These queer-heads, where they comin' from?' They had no worries. No worries in the world! It bothered me.

"The place scared me, too. Well, we stood there for a week and I wanted to go home. So we came home—and it looked as if God didn't want me to leave that ranch, because I was home one hour and I had trouble with the police. We had a fight . . . a little scramble! Before you know it, they had a warrant out for my arrest.

"First thing, I turn to this fellow and ask to go back to Colorado.

I got back there and a lot of things run through my mind. Then I decided—no! God decided to put Himself in my heart. I felt Him there, I knew He was there.

"When I came home, I had to go to court and I got sentenced. I prayed when I got sentenced. I just hoped and prayed, and God came through. This last time I was sentenced to six months and with the good Lord's help, I was out in six weeks.

"Now, my before and after. The first part was my bein' tough. You had to be tough. Nobody could push me around, I'm a big man, see! But now I want to respect people and have them respect me. Before, my reputation was to be a big shot. Now I want my reputation to say, 'There's Zeke. He's a nice boy. He's gonna get married. He's gonna raise a nice family.'

"I'm working. I didn't wanta work. Work was out, strictly out. I wanted the money but I didn't want the job. Now I'm working steady. To tell you the truth, I kinda like it a little bit.

"Well, what I gotta do now is thank the Lord for looking after me. And I thank you people for listening tonight."

The testimony of the ex-hoodlum Zeke was a part of Teen Week at the Garden. Teen Week was Graham's answer to the spate of vicious, senseless crimes that shocked and sickened New York in midsummer. Because of it boys and girls and their parents were attending the Garden in probably the greatest outpouring of young people in the modern church's history.

It had really started on the night that Graham was moved to issue a special challenge to the young people in his audience. His subject was "Youth Aflame." "Christ didn't call us to a picnic," he said. "Christ called us to a battle." He asked that all who would dedicate their lives completely to Christ and be ready to "go anywhere and do anything" to come forward. Over one thousand young people responded.

The stunning fact lay in his mind even while he wrote other sermons.

Suddenly the headlines of every Manhattan paper were dripping with the gore of teen-age violence. Their crimes were brutal, senseless, and malevolent. Newsboys screamed "Teen-agers on Crime Spree!" "Kid Killers on Rampage!" "Teen Gangs Wage War!" The city gasped, wondering what next.

Mayor Wagner appointed a committee to recommend emergency measures. Governor Harriman expressed official concern.

Graham went to the Garden that night with a burdened heart. There was a fatal sickness in the land, but its stench was stronger in Manhattan than anywhere else in the world.

He told a secretary, "After the service, get the team together and all the members of the executive committee you can find."

In his dressing room they talked until almost midnight, perfecting a new assault on Satan that would perhaps help straighten out New York's juvenile-delinquency mess. Graham would junk the sermons he had intended to preach. It was time to propose a program of Christian action.

This is the sort of midstream switch that has always distinguished Graham's ministry. When he feels led to a new course, he moves.

Researchers gathered facts. Youth today. Youth in the time of Christ. Youth in church, school and jail. Youth at home and abroad.

His program took shape. Services would be changed to appeal primarily to young people. Contacting teen-age gang leaders, he urged them to bring their members to the Garden. He wrote about juvenile delinquency for the New York press. He invited popular disk jockeys to help fill the Garden with rock-and-roll fans.

He held a press conference and showed how Christ had already worked in the hearts of a dozen youngsters with doubtful backgrounds. Twelve of them flanked him, some from a Christian summer camp. Several had court records.

Bill, age nineteen, was typical:

"I was with a gang, stealing, fighting, drinking. One day I met a counselor who offered me a vacation at this camp in the Adirondacks. One week for free, what could I lose? I went up and it was on an island in a big lake. We had no smokes, no beer, no juke box. And we were completely surrounded by water and I couldn't get away. These things I resented.

"Then a counselor gave me the idea that maybe somebody did care for me. His name was God. He said God loved me. This was news. That night, like he said, I knelt by my cot and prayed. It was not logical, but I prayed. After a while, I found that God really did love me and then he helped me to win out over my bad habits. One month after I accepted Jesus, my father and our whole family of nine kids turned to God just like I'd done."

By itself, such a statement by a young ex-hooligan was not news.

If it could be multiplied, perhaps by thousands, it would be very good news indeed.

Graham announced that crusade figures already showed 13,520 young people between the ages of twelve and eighteen who had made decisions. Next week, he promised, there would be many more.

Canceling all engagements, the evangelist retired to his room to work on as crucial a series of sermons as he had ever delivered. His diary, already neglected, became a memory.

Preaching during Teen Week, his manner changed to fit his younger audience.

He said, "I know a woman who has a no-good boy and she's trying to bring him up with love and kindness. One day she told me she didn't believe in whippings; instead, she always gave her boy a pat on the back. I said, 'Madam, if it's low enough and hard enough, it might do some good.'"

In addition to the sermon, two teen-agers testified each night, just as Zeke, who told of finding Christ at a dude ranch, had done. Members of a high-school society called Hi-BA were introduced. B for born. A for again. High-School Born-Againers!

Music was planned for young tastes. The Ohman Brothers, a trumpet trio, came from a youth camp; and the White Sisters, who had left show business after a turn at night clubs and the Arthur Godfrey show to enter full-time Christian work.

Platform guests were persons particularly admired by young men; Carl Erskine, pitcher for the Brooklyn Dodgers; Lou Nova, former boxer; Red Barber, sportscaster and lay preacher; Olympic star Andy Stanfield.

The tune was different but the words were the same. "The root of the trouble is sin," Graham preached. "Sin produces boredom, mischief, gang wars. But there is no boredom in a life dedicated to Christ."

One night he said, "I do not blame the teen-agers. Their difficulties stem from the environment we have created for them. We are beginning to reap what has been sown in the past generation. We've been taught the philosophy of the Devil, who says: 'Do as you please! Sow the wind.' And now we are reaping the whirlwind."

His advice to parents:

"Take time with your children! They long and hunger for it.

Be a pal, love them, spend hours with them. Make the center of your social life the home.

"Give your children ideals for living. Teach them moral and spiritual principles from the very beginning.

"Plan things together as a family . . . family socials, picnics.

"Discipline your children! The Bible teaches that parents are to discipline their children. Proverbs 29:17 says: 'Correct thy son, and he shall give thee rest.' If you fail, then you are breaking the laws, commandments and statutes of God.

"Teach your children to know God and bring them to church. Only about 4 per cent of juvenile delinquency comes from children reared in homes where church attendance is a necessity and Bible reading and prayer occur daily. Christ gives the moral stability, the understanding, wisdom, and patience necessary to rear children."

Another night he said, "Hitler got German youth to march proudly under the swastika. Mussolini got the youth of Italy to follow him in black shirts. The Communists are giving their youth a sense of dedication in the same way. *In America, let's give our youth Christ, and watch them march under his proud banner. Do that and the heart of the teen-age problem will be solved.*"

Headlines like these blossomed all over America:

"Graham Raps Parents for Teen Evils" . . . "Young People Need Control, Graham Says" . . . "Teeners Coddled, Bored, Need Dedication to Christ" . . . "Graham Urges Teen Gangs for Christ."

New Yorkers began to write their editors letters like these: To the *Herald Tribune:* "I was riding on a subway train. A group of seven teen-agers, going home from the crusade, were singing hymns in beautiful harmony. I thought what a contrast that was to the headlines I read earlier about the young man beaten by a gang. Teen-age hymn singers do not make the headlines so I would like to salute all the good youth of New York through those seven."

To the *World-Telegram & Sun:* "To cope with teen-age delinquency: Take such youngsters to listen to Billy Graham!"

The *Journal-American* editorialized: "Billy Graham is right. The cost of parental failure to discipline children and teach them religious faith is to 'reap what has been sown,' and this is the unvarnished truth of a challenging matter."

The Paterson, N. J., *Call* said: "The inspired evangelist, a fa-

ther of youngsters himself, has proposed a four way attack. They
are: rededication by parents to the job of being just parents; re-
opening churches in summer and all the year round; renewing
Bible reading in the schools; revising the child labor law with
a view to giving more young people gainful and constructive
occupation.

"Here is advice from America's greatest evangelist that should
be taken to heart by the people of New York City and by every
municipality in the nation."

At the end of Teen Week there was a time of rejoicing. The
devil, if not routed, was in retreat and now one could rest.

Not yet, said Graham!

He turned to the High School Evangelism Fellowship, which
sponsors the High-School Born-Again clubs. With ten centers
in metropolitan New York, they could undertake a thorough
follow-up.

Brandt Reed, general director, explained their work:

"Our purpose is the salvation of high-school students, helping
them to a way of Christian living, and finding God's way for their
lives. When we hear of a teen-ager who has made a decision, we
get the name and address and give it to one of our staff. He rounds
up some of his Hi-BA kids who've been crusade-trained as counselors. For example, a staff member with a car may be given
twelve names. If they are girls, he will take a couple of Hi-BA
girl counselors with him. He'll drive them to the address and they
make the contact."

Results? These are reports from staffers.

"My inquirer had just left for camp, but her mother told me
she had been very zealous. She took not only her own small Bible
to camp but insisted on taking the mother's big Bible as well."

Another: "This boy made his decision in the Garden. He was
seventeen and lived on the top floor of a ramshackle building. The
hall was dark and dungeon-like. We learned that he had not done
his Bible lessons because he could neither read nor write English.
His mother was so cordial and happy that *somebody* in the big
city had cared enough to come and visit her son."

Another: "We contacted this boy, thirteen years old. He is so
filled with the Spirit that he took along seven or eight of his friends
to other Garden meetings. We made arrangements for them to
enroll in a nearby Sunday school."

Another: "This boy I contacted, he already led his whole family to Christ. We're seeing that they meet the pastor of a church of their choice."

At the end of Teen Week in the Garden over two thousand youngsters had come forward to surrender their lives. Nor was that the end; suddenly, in countless homes and communities, parents, friends, and neighbors began to learn at first hand what Billy Graham meant when he said, "You can be born again."

17 *The heart of Billy Graham's proclamation was the good news that man can be born again...*

John Wesley, who founded the Methodist Church, had preached the same doctrine. So had many other great revivalists. Once upon a time, most theologians thought it included a physical manifestation in which the body of the "born-againer" shook or trembled.

The Society of Friends in England got its name when its converts began to shake and quake, and the populace derided them as "quakers."

Conversion was frequently so violent that men and women fell to the floor as if dead and remained in a trancelike fit for hours. Evangelists of those days usually exhorted their listeners, not to come forward, but to "Fall down! Fall down! Surrender your soul to the Lord."

Whatever its embodiment, from the tremblings that possessed the citizens of a forgotten century to the simple act of the will (which may or may not be accompanied by emotion) of a modern Graham crusade, all were nourished by the concept of being spiritually born again.

Graham tried often to explain it. It became part of almost every sermon. But no effort was so successful and no explanation so clear as the sermon he preached very early in the crusade, from the text that said:

152

"There was a man named Nicodemus, a ruler of the Jews. The same came to Jesus by night, and said unto Him, Rabbi, we know that thou art a teacher come from God, for no man can do these miracles that thou doest, except God be with him. Jesus answered and said unto him, 'Verily, verily, I say unto thee, except a man be born of water and of the Spirit he cannot enter into the Kingdom of God.'"

Here are Graham's words, condensed slightly, as the audience heard them in the Garden:

Have you been born again? And are you certain? Do you know? If I didn't know I had been born again, you couldn't drag me out of Madison Square Garden until I had settled it. This is not some theory or philosophy of mine. These are the words of Jesus. He said, "Ye must be born again."

What did Jesus mean by that?

First of all, I want you to see the necessity of being born again. A little boy one day had been in trouble over many things. When reprimanded by his mother he said, "I guess I was just born wrong." He spoke more truly than he realized. There's something wrong with the whole human race. Pick up your newspaper; have you ever seen so much crime, so much raping, so much wickedness, so much immorality, so much robbery, so much murder? Certainly there's something wrong.

What is it?

Well, the psychiatrist, the psychoanalyst, and even world leaders are trying to diagnose man's problems. I think I told you about the young doctor who hung out his sign. His first patient came in and gave all of his symptoms. The young doctor couldn't figure it out so he went into an inner office to study his books. Finally he came out and very nervously said, "Sir, would you mind giving me the symptoms again?" The old man gave him the symptoms again, but the doctor still couldn't diagnose it.

He said, "Sir, have you ever had this disease before?"

The old man said, "Why yes, I have."

The young doctor said, "Well, you've got it again!"

And that is about as far as the world has gotten in analyzing its problems, and diagnosing its disease. We have got the same old problems that they had back in Napoleon's time, the same old problem they had in Julius Caesar's time, the same old problem that they had in the days of Achilles and Ulysses. Fashions change, languages change, civilization changes, but the human heart remains the same. Out of it comes lying, cheating, hating, and prejudice. All of these things come from within and the Bible says we have a disease called sin, all of us are infected.

We have an old type of germ called sin. It is a disease that eats out the soul and the heart, until you end in destruction and hell. It is the disease called sin that separates between you and God. The Bible says in Isaiah 1:6, "From the sole of the foot even unto the head, there is no soundness in it, but wounds and bruises and putrefying sores, they have not been closed, neither bound up, neither mollified with ointment."

Jeremiah 17:9 says, "The heart is deceitful above all things and desperately wicked, who can know it?"

Romans 3:23: "For all have sinned and come short of the Glory of God."

Romans 5:12: "Wherefore, as by one man sin entereth into the world and death by sin; and so death passed upon all men for that all have sinned."

Job said, "Behold, I am vile and I abhor myself."

Peter said, "Depart from me for I am a sinful man."

All of us are sinful. Every one of us has broken God's law. We have failed to keep His Commandments. We've come short of His Glory. We have a disease that the Bible calls "Sin." That means that we need a new nature, our old nature is sinful. The old nature of the best of us is bad in the sight of God. The old nature of Nicodemus was corrupt. On the outside he was fine, gracious, courteous, religious; nevertheless within he was corrupt. Jesus said, Nicodemus, what you need is a new heart, a new nature, a new direction in your life. You need a new beginning, a new birth!

You ask, what is a new birth? What does it mean to be born again?

A certain twelve-year-old was going to write an essay on the topic "birth." He went to his mother and said, "Mother, where did I come from?" She replied, "Why, the stork brought you." He then said, "Mother, where did you come from?" She answered, "Why the stork brought me." He went to his grandmother and said, "Grandmother, where did you come from?" She said, "The stork brought me." His essay began with these words, "There

hasn't been a natural birth in this family in three generations."
What is this new birth? What is this being born again?

Jesus said, "That which is born of flesh is flesh." That means that you were born from your mother in the physical world. Then Jesus said, "That which is born of spirit is spirit." So you must be born into God's family by birth. You don't grow into God's family. You don't reform your way into God's family. You don't moralize your way into God's family. You don't intellectualize your way or rationalize your way into God's family. You are born into God's family.

Have you been born into the family of God? The whole Bible teaches that everyone must be born again or be eternally lost. Ezekiel 36:26 says, "A new heart also will I give you and a new spirit will I put within you."

John called it being born of the spirit, born of God, born from above.

Peter calls it an act of repenting and being converted and says we are "born again by the Word of God which liveth and abideth."

Paul speaks of it in Romans as being alive from the dead and in II Corinthians he calls it being a "new creature, old things have passed away, behold, all things become new." In Ephesians he speaks of it as being quickened, of being made alive, from the dead. In Colossians, Paul calls it a putting off of the old man with his doings and putting on the new man, which is the new creation. In Titus he calls it the working of regeneration and the renewing of the Holy Ghost.

In Peter, the Apostle said, "being made partakers of the divine nature."

In the Epistle of John, he calls it passing from death unto life.

In the Church of England catechism the Anglicans and Episcopalians have called this "A death unto sin and a new birth unto righteousness."

Every denomination, every catechism, teaches something about the matter of the new birth. Different terminology may be used, but the facts are always there. We that have been born the first time into the physical world can be born the second time, we can be changed, translated into the Kingdom of God.

I ask you again, Have you been born anew? Have you been born from above? Have you entered into the Kingdom of God by the new birth?

To be born anew doesn't mean to be altered, doesn't mean to be influenced, or reinvigorated, or reformed or feel a little better. It's an entirely new beginning when we take on a family likeness to God. The Scripture teaches us that it is not merely a reformation. A man may quit his meanness, he may turn over a new leaf, he may reform, but that's not enough. Just a New Year's resolution will never do. That's not the new birth.

There are many people that have the idea that they don't need to be born again and that they are still going to get to heaven. But if you haven't been born again, you'd be out of place in heaven. Take a fish out of the ocean, put him in your living room, put him on a beautiful soft chair, and let somebody fan him because it's warm. Put a little perfume on him to make him smell good. Do everything in the world for him, but the fish will soon feel a little uncomfortable sitting on your living-room chair. Why? Because the fish belongs in water. He was made for water.

If you could take a sinner to heaven, he'd be out of place too. Heaven would be hell on earth to some of you. You're so used to kicking your heels down here and going your own way, you'd get up to heaven and you'd be totally out of place. You must have a new nature if you're to be accepted by God. If you're to have fellowship with God and Christ and the angels and the Apostles and the great men of God, you must have a divine nature. You cannot cure a tree by giving it new bark and some new branches; there must be new sap. Suppose I saw a man building a wooden ship and he was building it out of rotten timber. You can't build a character fit for the kingdom of heaven out of the rotten timber of your old heart and your old deceitful nature. You have to be born again.

Man cannot generate within himself that quality of life that will gain him entrance into the kingdom of heaven, it must come from above, from God. It's more than a change of environment. I've got a watch that doesn't work but I don't know why. All right, I say to myself, I wear my watch on my right arm but it's not working. I tell you what this watch needs. It needs a different arm. I'll put it on my left arm and I know it will work. I'll give it a change of environment. But the watch still lies to me. There's something wrong inside of the watch. Its works need to be fixed.

Now, I give you a change of environment, but you're still the same. You need an operation down inside, and that operation is done by the Holy Spirit. It is called the new birth.

Many people protest, saying, I had Christian parents and I've been reared in the Church. Isn't that enough?

No! You can't inherit it. It doesn't come from the flesh and blood. It's not a physical change. This birth does not add to or subtract from your intellectual emotional and voluntary faculties. The new birth gives a new direction to your affections. You might have loved before, but your love was set on yourself. After the new birth, you will love with all your heart, soul, and mind your neighbor as yourself. The new birth is a change of direction and a change of affection. It's a union of the soul with Christ. Christ comes to you through the Holy Spirit and you become a partaker of God's life.

You see, originally man and God were together. But sin came and separated God and man. When Christ came to die on the Cross, He rose again; and lives to bring you and me, who were dead in trespasses and sin, back into the life of God, so that spiritual life can begin to flow once again.

As soon as I receive Christ as Savior, spiritual life like spiritual sap begins to flow through me. I have the capacity to love. I have a new joy and a new peace. My whole life has changed. There's a new spring in my step and a new joy in my soul.

Yes, there will be problems. He doesn't remove your problems. Your problems may be even greater after you come to Christ, but you will have a capacity and power to face them. You have a new life, you have God's life. The Bible says that God is from everlasting to everlasting. Therefore the moment you receive Christ you are grafted into the life of God and you live as long as God lives. Your body will die and go to the grave, but the real you, your personality, your soul, your intelligence, your memory lives on forever in God. You are adopted into the family of God.

That is what happens in the new birth.

Have you been born again?

You may say, "How do we get this new birth?" Nicodemus asked the same question. He said, "How can these things be?" Henry Clay once said that he did not know for himself personally what the change of heart spoken of by Christians meant. But he had seen Kentucky family feuds of long standing healed by religious revival, and he said that whatever could heal a family feud

157

was more than human, and I agree with Henry Clay. It is more than human. It is a divine act.

The Bible says, "Being born again not of the corruptible seed but of the incorruptible by the Word of God which liveth and abideth forever."

The Bible says, "Faith cometh by hearing, and hearing by the Word of God." I preach to you tonight the truth, the Word of God. You hear it, you receive it into your hearts and the moment you are willing to receive it in repentance and by faith, at that moment the Holy Spirit does His regenerating work.

Now the whole operation of the new birth is done by the Holy Spirit. You have no power to make yourself born into the family of God. The Bible says in John 1:12, you can't just come up and say to God, God I want to be born again today. It doesn't come to pass that way. You can come only when the Holy Spirit draws you. The Bible teaches that the Holy Spirit convinces of sin, you must know that you are a sinner first.

If you know that you have failed God, that you've broken His laws, that you've failed to live up to the Sermon on the Mount, that you have failed to live like Christ, then that is the Holy Spirit convicting you of the fact that you are a sinner.

That's the first step to the Kingdom of God. "No man can come to me except the Father draw him," says Jesus.

When you feel miserable inside and know that you are guilty, and sense that you are a sinner in the sight of God, you should rejoice because that is the Holy Spirit convicting you of your need of the Savior. No man can come to the Savior without first knowing that he is a sinner.

And then the Bible says, "The Holy Spirit prepares the heart." Just as the farmer breaks up the soil for the planting of seeds, so the Holy Spirit opens the heart and prepares the heart and then He draws you to the Savior.

But this you must know. You can reject the wooing of the Holy Spirit, if you choose. Many of you are doing that. The Holy Spirit says that you should come to Christ, but you resist. Your pride gets in the way. You say, "Well, if I openly receive Christ, what will people think?" Your pride makes you resist.

It may be some moral sin that you don't want to give up. It may be some stand that you know you'll have to take in your community. Or some witness you'll have to give in your office or shop. You are afraid you will be unpopular, so you resist the Holy Spirit.

I want to warn you. The Holy Spirit moves in like a tide, then moves out, and you had better come to Christ when the wind of the Spirit is blowing. Jesus said, "The wind bloweth where it listeth." Jesus used the word "wind." "The wind bloweth where it will, so is everyone that is born of the Spirit."

I want you to notice that the wind is sovereign. The wind is an element altogether independent and uncontrollable. The wind doesn't consult us when it wants to blow. It is not regulated by our wishes. So it is with the Spirit. "The wind bloweth where it listeth," where it pleases, when it pleases, and as it pleases. You can't direct the Holy Spirit. Then, the wind is irresistible. When a tornado comes, who can stand before it? When the Holy Spirit comes, if we will allow Him, He breaks down a man's prejudice. He subdues his rebellious will. He overcomes all opposition.

The wind is variable. Sometimes it moves so softly that it scarcely rustles the leaves. At other times it blows so that its roar can be heard for miles. So is the manner of the Holy Spirit in the act of regeneration. For some people He works so gently that His work is not observed by onlookers. With others He is actually so forceful and evident that one can never doubt or forget the moment or the manner of His coming.

There is unlimited variety and freshness of expression in the operation of the Holy Spirit. The wind is mysterious. It defies all human explanation. So the Holy Spirit's operation is conducted secretly. That is the reason no one can fully explain to you the new birth. I may explain it in part, but it is a mysterious operation of the Holy Spirit.

I do not understand how a man can get up on his feet in some distant part of this auditorium and come here and say that he is renouncing his sin and is receiving Christ and be changed in an instant to be acceptable to God because of Christ who died on the Cross.

But I know it happens. It's the mysterious operation of the Holy Spirit. This is the one thing some reporters have difficulty with. They cannot understand this mysterious element, the regenerating power of the Holy Spirit and how a life is made over. There are many men and women that are new persons in Christ Jesus, but they can't explain it.

You can't analyze it. You can't perfectly describe it! You just know you have been changed. The blind man (whose eyes Jesus had opened) couldn't explain a thing. When the Pharisees asked what had happened to him, he said, "I don't know. Once I was blind, now I can see."

The Bible teaches that the wind is indispensable. If a dead calm would continue indefinitely, vegetation would die. Even more so is it with the Spirit. Without Him there could be no spiritual life at all.

The Bible teaches that the wind is invigorating. Its life giving properties are illustrated every time a physician orders his sick patient to retire to the mountains or to the seaside and get some of that fresh air.

You come to Jesus Christ tonight and give Him your life. He will invigorate you. He will give you a new life and new power, a new thrill to living. He transforms and changes, and makes you a new Christian. And it's the work of the Spirit. It's a divine act upon the soul.

I'm convinced that conversion is a process. There might have been a long process bringing you to the moment of decision, and there should be a process of growth after the decision is made, but I am convinced that the new birth is instantaneous. It is the operation in a moment of the Holy Spirit. It can happen to you now! The moment you repent and believe.

Are you sure that you've been born again?

If not, let Him change your life now, and make you a new creation in Christ. Are you sure that you've been forgiven? Are you certain that if you died you'd go to heaven?

In Florence, Italy, near the church of Santa Maria Novella, there lay a huge block of marble. Sculptor after sculptor had tried but had failed to achieve anything. It had been chiseled and hammered until it was shapeless. At last Michelangelo was commissioned to take it in hand. Over this stone he built a house and then he went in and locked the door. For eighteen months he worked and nobody could see him.

At last the citizens were admitted and out of that mass that the other sculptors had disfigured, the sublime figure of David, which is now the glory of Florence, emerged.

Christ can take lives that sin has distorted, and transform them into His likeness.

Will you let Him? You may say, "Well, Billy, what do I have to do?"

You must say to God, "I am a sinner and I renounce my sins." You must say to Christ tonight, "I receive you as Lord and Savior. I'm willing to deny myself and take up the Cross and follow you, whatever the cost. I want to be yours, I want to be born into the family of God, now."

Have you ever taken that step? You may be a member of the church or you may not be. You may be religious and good, or you may be like the thief on the cross. You may be Jew or Gentile. I'm asking you to come and give your life to Christ, and be born into His family. Have your sins forgiven and become a new creation in Christ.

This is the way we're going to do it. I'm going to ask you to come quietly and reverently and stand here. We'll have a moment of prayer and a verse of Scripture. We'll give you some literature before you go. If you're with friends and relatives, they will wait for you.

You may wonder why I ask you to come forward. Jesus said, "If you don't confess me before men, I'll not confess you before my Father which is in Heaven." There is something about coming forward which settles it, but, more than that, it is an act of your will in receiving Christ.

Jesus could have healed the man with the withered arm by saying, "Be healed." But he didn't do it. Jesus said to him, "Stretch it forth." The man looked at Jesus and, upon the authority of the word of God, he stretched it forth. And he was healed!

I'm asking you to stretch your life forth and commit it to Christ. Surrender your life to Him to serve and to follow Him. Let Him wash your sins away and make you a new creation.

I'm going to ask men, women, young people all over the building to come and stand quietly here. I'm not asking you to join some organization.

"I'm asking you to come to Christ. Not to me. I'm not giving the invitation, it's the Holy Spirit that gives the invitation. We are the ambassadors on behalf of Christ, as though God were entreating by us. We beseech you, on behalf of Christ, be ye reconciled to God.

18

Men have a way, once a thing is done, of shrugging it off. "Easy," they say. "Nothing to it." Some at the Garden thought that, too. But behind each sermon, each service, each decision lay the crusade's master plan . . .

Facing his last Garden audience, Billy Graham analyzed the New York Crusade. "What brought about these transformations of lives among people of both high and low estate?" he asked. "Here is the answer. First of all, it happened because there's an innate cry for God in the heart of man. We were made in God's image and man is restless until he finds God.

"Secondly, we are living in a period of revolt against secularism and materialism. Our materialistic culture does not satisfy the longings of the human heart.

"Thirdly, there is a nationwide disillusionment with other philosophies.

"Fourthly, we are living in a period of world crisis when so-called human progress is bringing us face to face with the hydrogen bomb and with guided missiles which can destroy great segments of our civilization.

"But there are still more specific reasons . . . there has been world-wide prayer . . . there has been great unity among the churches . . . God has used a consecrated organization of dedicated men and women who have been working behind the scenes . . . there is the sovereignty of God . . . there has been the Gospel of Christ presented with authority and simplicity."

A consultant on business management would undoubtedly agree with Dr. Graham on every point. But he would also lift out one of his sentences and give to it considerably greater emphasis.

That sentence? "God has used a consecrated organization of dedicated men and women who have been working behind the scenes." In short, the consultant would give more credit to the crusade executive committee, the Graham team, and his staff.

Business management has been called the use of wealth to create products or services and find customers for them. Billy Graham took a product called a Fuller brush, when he was a high-school boy, and went through both Carolinas looking for customers.

More than any modern minister, he recognizes that the Church's evangelistic mission, to succeed in this century, must follow contemporary marketing practices. In some minds, this makes him a religious huckster. By whatever name, he gets a hearing. Despite the expensive clamor of TV, movies, radio, baseball, football, Rock-and-Roll, bridge, bingo, and the continuing thunder of H-bomb tests, he gets a hearing for God's word.

Insurance-company ads offer leisure, early retirement, and old-age security. Air-line advertisements offer romantic holidays in exotic lands. They are selling ideas and nothing but ideas. The idea Billy Graham offers is new birth, new strength, divine guidance, escape from hell, peace and satisfaction, and the promise of life beyond the grave. He finds it defined in the Bible.

That is quite a package.

By any reasonable ethic, Graham is completely correct in presenting it to the public with the same dignity, efficiency, and regard for the common good that characterizes the marketing practices of any reputable business.

A Graham lieutenant once said, "A businessman can spend fifteen million dollars a year to persuade people to smoke or wash themselves and there's no criticism. But let a minister spend a million offering eternal life to people and he gets kicked all over the lot."

The miracle of Graham's ministry is that he is able, despite considerable reliance upon the gadgetry of communications, to create in stadium, ball park, or Cow Palace the reverent atmosphere of a cathedral, and to project his own spirituality so effectively that there is no hint of claptrap theatricality or sawdust emotionalism.

A crusade is many things to many people, and what Graham sees one way might be viewed by others in a different light. He referred to activities behind the scenes. Hereafter, with no attempt to be exhaustive, are many of the items to which he alluded.

Graham's original agreement with every crusade committee embraced two firm items. First, all money would be collected and disbursed by a committee of New Yorkers, and no Graham team member would have anything to do with it. Second, the starting date would be May 15, 1957.

Jerry Beavan, executive secretary of the organization, was the first man to arrive. He opened an office at 165 West Forty-sixth Street, just off Broadway, on May 1, 1956.

His equipment was an old table left by a previous tenant. His typewriter was the "portable" he had carried around the world. His assistant was Ruth Campbell, a secretary in the Hollywood offices of World Wide Pictures who made herself available to the New York Crusade when other Graham staff members were engaged elsewhere.

The immediate order of business in New York was to set up the first of several committees, a hard-working group to be known as the Crusade Executive Committee.

For chairman, all agreed upon Roger Hull, a prominent Presbyterian of Darien, Connecticut, and executive vice-president of Mutual of New York, an insurance firm. At various times it also named these nineteen distinguished men to serve with him: Erling C. Olsen, Edwin F. Chinlund, Dr. John S. Bonnell, George Champion, Cleveland E. Dodge, Reverend Ralph C. Drisko, Dr. Phillips P. Elliott, Reverend Richard L. Francis, Dr. Frank Gaebelein, Dr. Richard Hildebrand, Reverend Frederick G. Hubach, Howard E. Isham, J. Turner Jones, Reverend Lloyd Lee, Ralph M. McDermid, Dr. Louis W. Pitt, Dr. Gardner C. Taylor, Honorable Charles H. Tuttle, Dr. John S. Wimbish.

Other committees would be needed later for innumerable crusade operations; a prayer committee, music committee, ushers' committee, committee for counseling and follow-up, ministerial committee, arrangements committee, extension and delegation committee, and they would come in due course.

Immediately the size and weight of New York made itself felt. The city was too big and too sprawling and too populous. It became particularly evident in the organization of prayer and of counselor training.

"We had to break the city into eleven sections, and handle each one separately," Beavan explained later. "We found we were not just organizing one crusade. We were organizing eleven elements which would converge at the same time and place."

Each of these committees immediately multiplied into eleven area committees with their own chairmen and programs of activities.

Two matters needed immediate attention. Funds with which to meet crusade expenses. A program of information for local pastors about the significance and potential of a Billy Graham Crusade.

A finance committee took over the fund-raising task.

The Graham team assumed the burden of telling its story throughout the metropolitan area. Again, they underestimated the weight of the world's biggest city. Beavan asked for assistance in the task of telling the story to ministers. Charles Riggs and Leighton Ford were sent to New York to help. After calling on scores of pastors, they decided that Uncle Sam's mailmen would have to carry the message. A great mailing campaign was begun.

What would the crusade cost? Businessmen on the Executive Committee wanted to know. "Make up a budget," they told Beavan.

Behind lay the experience of nearly forty other crusades.

In Nashville, the budget had been eighty thousand dollars.

In London, where labor and rents and printing costs were half of New York's prices, the committee had spent about $425,000.

The first budget, for six and a half weeks in the Garden and for the preparation, was for an expenditure of approximately $900,000.

If the crusade were extended beyond that date, it would cost the committee an additional $56,600 per week.

Items:

Garden rental, per week	$33,000
Advertising, per week	10,000
Office operation, per week	3,000
Team housing, per week	2,500
Specialized staff housing	2,100
Follow-up	2,000
Miscellaneous	2,000

Revisions followed, additions were voted, and then television reared its expensive head. The financial aspect of the crusade was the subject of a special story in the New York *Times* immediately after the opening. It said:

"None of the coins or folding money that New Yorkers dropped into paper buckets at Madison Square Garden last night goes to line the pockets of the Rev. Dr. Billy Graham or the members of what he calls his 'team.'

"The offering, collected with the same streamlined efficiency that characterizes all the Graham operations, goes toward meeting the local expenses of the New York Crusade.

"The evangelist's men do not even touch the money. It is handled by local people working under Edwin F. Chinlund, treasurer of the crusade. He is also a vice president and treasurer of R. H. Macy, Inc.

"The crusades are incorporated locally and the purse strings are controlled locally. Dr. Graham and his staff receive only their housing and living expenses in the host city.

"For the New York Crusade, $39,500, out of a total budget of $1,300,000, has been allotted for these expenses over six and one-half weeks. Dr. Graham's staff for the crusade here numbers thirty-five. His personal suite at the New Yorker Hotel has been given without charge by the hotel.

"The other major expenses for the crusade here are $400,000 for Saturday night telecasts of the meetings, starting June 1; $360,000 for the use of Madison Square Garden, $255,000 for promotion, $105,000 for office expenses and $100,000 for contingencies.

"The collections to be taken up at the Garden every night are expected to bring in only $250,000 toward the budget. The balance is expected to be met by contributions from individuals and organizations solicited by mail or television."

The story mentioned the housing expense of the Graham team. What does it cost a man who is away from home to live decently in a mid-town hotel? The committee voted a per diem allowance of fifteen dollars.

During those early months, Beavan moved to a new hotel each week, testing their facilities as a possible home for the Graham team. Ministers, no matter how young and rugged, cannot live in a slum, nor can they patronize a glamor-type hotel without being criticized. Somewhere in the middle, he hoped to find a hostelry with an efficient switchboard, good service, and enough room to keep team members from running over each other.

He found what he wanted at the Hotel New Yorker, which soon became the team home. Ultimately, because of that choice, there would come one night during the crusade when over a thousand of its rooms would be filled by Graham aids, friends, and enthusiasts.

As other members of the team came to town, they began to report that few New Yorkers knew what took place in a Graham crusade. And that included the ministers who were being asked to co-operate. So young Bill Brown, another halfback type, was hurried to Manhattan with a film library. Using motion pictures of earlier crusades, Brown soon had screenings scheduled for hundreds of churches, clubs, and homes throughout the area.

New York is traditionally an eight-thirty town. Everything starts at eight-thirty: theaters, fights, hockey, basketball. The idea of starting the Garden service at seven-thirty seemed shocking at first.

In its favor were several unanswerable facts. Movie houses, when they had a hit, were full at seven-thirty. An early service encouraged parents to bring their children; old folks, too, who could get home to bed at a reasonable hour.

So the early opening was adopted, but several reluctant committeemen kept their fingers crossed until the decision was approved by history.

Introducing a crusade to the public requires an advertising program and policy. Decisions are made on the basis of experience, knowledge of crowd habits, mass movement of people to and from work, reading preferences, and media effectiveness. Each final decision must be tempered by the funds available.

London had been placarded months in advance, under a policy of letting the news sink in slowly. New York's tempo was different. New York lives from explosion to explosion. Its approval or disapproval can be volcanic. Then it forgets, fast.

The policy adopted for New York packed the power of the entire ad budget in a hard-hitting "blast-off" campaign prior to opening night.

Committeemen like to know who does what. Committeemen are just as ignorant, in the beginning, as is the general public.

Even newsmen who had never attended a crusade meeting had no idea of the scope and outreach of the evangelist's mission.

So job descriptions were written for all key positions. One is typical of all. This one presents the duties of Leighton Ford, Director of Pastoral Relations:

"The Director of Pastoral Relations works as liaison between the staff and the New York church leadership to study the religious situation, interpret crusade objectives and plans to local leaders, inform and inspire churches regarding plans.

"He will prepare a study of the religious situation of the Greater New York area showing:

"Number of churches by denomination

"Number of members by denomination

"Statistics on church attendance

"Problems and difficulties faced by local groups

"Pertinent population statistics of racial groups

"He will contact all denomination headquarters, and leaders for the area. He will seek their guidance on the best approach to their churches.

"He will visit each church council in the area.

"He will visit individual ministers to get their help.

"He will speak before every group of ministers possible, to explain and inspire.

"He will evalute the response of denominations and areas, and program further efforts.

"He will arrange, where needed, special conferences for Dr. Graham with representative ministers and leaders prior to the crusade.

"He will set up ministers' seminars to take place during the crusade.

"He will devise means of telling ministers how best to integrate their programs into crusade plans."

The worry about money was never ending. This, however, was a committee worry, not the team's. They were the committee's guests, and the host footed the bills. In New York a professional fund raiser was hired for a short time. Committee members solicited their friends for funds. A dinner was given in September of 1956 to introduce Graham to 1200 church leaders and money men. Afterward, many of those guests contributed substantially in cash and in pledges.

Windfall gifts came from other cities, sites of recent crusades, which had surplus funds that were generously sent along to help preach the Gospel in New York. Louisville, Kentucky, contributed $22,000. Richmond sent $24,991. Many prayer groups around the country gave their mite, without solicitation.

As more team members arrived for special assignments, they began to make small disbursements. The committee established a policy to control expenses:

Departmental directors could approve $100.

The Administrative Director, to which spot Charles Riggs was eventually moved, could approve up to $1500.

Anything costing more than $1500 required the approval of the Executive Committee, its chairman, its treasurer, or secretary.

A committeeman suggested that the churches of New York should be asked to share expenses. The team position was that this should be undertaken only after all other means of raising funds were exhausted.

The committee asked the team how much might be expected in the way of contributions. Beavan answered that the average in other cities was about twenty-five cents per person. New York proved more generous, averaging better than thirty cents. Collections for the first four nights in the Garden were:

May 15, $9,123.

May 16, $6,600.

May 17, $7,659.

May 18, $7,768.

Odd items turned up in some collections. One child contributed a piggy bank full of dimes and pennies; someone else, an old salt box full of pennies.

A wallet was picked up and sent to the Lost and Found department. The woman in charge wrote to the man whose card she found. He replied, "Thank you. I'll appreciate getting the wallet and the papers but please take the nineteen dollars in it and drop it in the collection plate for me."

Headquarters began to bulge now with new arrivals, volunteer workers, and occasional visitors. Director of Office Services Ruth Campbell needed more secretarial help and could not find it. Miraculously, word spread by letter and telephone and suddenly girls from other crusade cities were volunteering their services. Two came from Oklahoma City, another came from Texas.

This did not surprise Miss Campbell, who was accustomed to miracles. One morning she had started to work with only four pennies and a fifty-dollar check in her purse. When she tried to cash her check with suspicious Manhattan storekeepers, they laughed at her. Subway fare was fifteen cents, and she had only four. Returning to her apartment, she opened her Bible and read, "I will go before thee; the Lord will provide."

It gave her the confidence she needed. By faith, she started again toward the subway. Her eyes saw a shimmering spot on the sidewalk ahead. She looked more closely, and then picked up a shiny new subway token. The Lord had provided.

A motto hanging on the wall of the headquarters conference room read, "We know that all things work together for good to them that love the Lord."

Sometimes there must have been doubt, particularly in the face of the tremendous mailings that were faced so often during those days by both hired help and volunteers.

In a crisis, they worked the clock around, from dusk until dawn, running mimeograph machines like a printing press, stuffing and addressing envelopes.

Two young ministerial students hitchhiked from California and spent their summer working in the office. A vice-president of one of the city's largest banks sent his family to Maine, reported each morning to Miss Campbell, and did whatever two extra hands could do.

A high-school superintendent did the same.

An able-bodied seaman, grizzled and tattooed, was converted at the Garden and canceled all his sailings so he could spend his days at work in the mail room.

The big problem, as in all New York offices, was getting the people in on time. An office bulletin carried this plaintive note: "Of late, we have been a little negligent with regard to arriving at the office by nine o'clock. Of late, we have started our morning prayer meeting with almost half of the staff missing."

Team and staff members observed an astonishing workday. Starting at nine, they went through the whole day, usually without leaving their desks for lunch. By seven or seven-fifteen, they were in duplicate offices at the Garden, carrying on with other

170

assigned duties. Most of the secretaries by day became counselors by night. Their day was rarely less than twelve to fourteen hours long.

As interest mounted, Director of Press Relations Betty Lowry conferred helpfully with a stream of writers from national weeklies, religious monthlies, and daily newspapers located from coast to coast. Preparing for the opening night, she issued press passes to qualified reporters and added their names to her mailing list.

Margaret Osborn, from Wales, with the experience of Harringay and Glasgow, moved in to help her. Later, Paul Keating from New Jersey would join her staff. As would Don Barnhouse, a Graham research assistant, to take charge of the crusade's daily newspaper, the *Crusade News,* which was distributed free each night at the Garden and mailed monthly to 175,000 prayer partners.

Recruiting for volunteers began early and lasted long. First counselors, then ushers, singers, and church delegations.

Again, the medium used was direct mail. Letter series were prepared based on extensive experience elsewhere, modified to fit the New York situation, and run through duplicating machines.

This typical series solicited singers:

1. Letter to a pastor asking him (or the church secretary) to list the names of his choir members who might sing in the crusade choir.

2. Letter to the pastor, asking him to name a music-committee member for his church.

3. Letter to the music committeeman asking for the names of possible choir members.

4. Letter to a singer (named by either of the foregoing) extending an invitation to sing in the crusade choir. A return card was enclosed, asking the recruit to indicate preference for the Monday-Wednesday-Friday or the Tuesday-Thursday-Saturday choir.

5. Another letter to the music committeeman saying that the opening was almost at hand and more names were desperately needed, asking for additional recommendations.

6. A letter to each singer thus far recruited asking him or her to enlist at least one friend.

7. A letter of instructions about attending any or all of three

rehearsals scheduled for May 9, May 11, and the Dedication Meeting in the Garden on May 14.

8. A letter issued during the crusade to each member, signed by Billy Graham, thanking the singer for past services, and asking for help on the final three weeks.

9. A certificate beautifully printed on heavy paper, saying: Certificate of Appreciation—in grateful recognition of outstanding service, this testimonial is awarded to Jane Doe, whose voluntary and wholehearted service has contributed so largely to the success of this historic crusade for Christ in New York City, signaling a new era in the lives of tens of thousands of people and strengthening the spiritual fiber of hundreds of churches in the New York area and across the nation. It was signed by Billy Graham and Roger Hull.

Special projects bloomed inside headquarters and out. Jean Graham, who is Billy's kid sister and the wife of associate evangelist Leighton Ford, became official receptionist in the outer office so that she could personally greet visitors, including the evangelist's old friends and acquaintances.

Marti Haymaker began offering help to those who asked about cheap rooms and lodging near the Garden. She visited restaurants and got discount cards for crusade visitors. She inspected hotels and rooming houses and made up three lists of rooms from five dollars and up, rooms for less than five dollars per day, and rooming houses with rooms for six to twelve dollars per week.

One of her correspondents was a woman who could pay only a little and who had to be alone, because she was a prayer missionary. She had attended fourteen earlier Graham crusades, ordered by the Lord to pray for Billy Graham, she said. Sometimes she prayed aloud all night, which made it disagreeable for anyone sharing a room with her.

After her arrival, she called Miss Haymaker to say triumphantly that the Lord had met her needs again. She was in a nice room close to the Garden, and the price was right. Of course, she had been forced to go in with another lady but even that turned out all right, because her roommate was stone deaf.

With the crusade under way, other projects multiplied.

Ministers' workshops were held to co-ordinate the work of local clergymen into an active evangelistic program. Workshops were held in eight areas, and subjects in each series were: Congregational Evangelism, Following up Evangelistic Decisions, the Theology of the Gospel, and Personal Evangelism.

Nightly Bible classes were undertaken by team members for the instruction of new Christians. They came by the thousands. On one memorable night Graham invited them all to a special Garden meeting where he spoke on the requirements of Christian living.

Through every day and night of the crusade, in addition to the preaching, there were the other endless chores: the daily radio prayer programs, the nightly "Impact" telecast, counseling by telephone, counseling in the Garden, counseling by mail, the weekly "Hour of Decision," millions of pieces of literature produced and distributed.

And through it all, there was the mounting pressure of the follow-up, the ultimate adhesive device by which the evangelist and his team seek to help each new Christian into the full realization of his born-again life.

And through it all, there was the steady drumbeat of publicity and promotion, which is the contemporary method of getting a hearing.

And through it all, there was the deft, sure managerial decisions of Graham's "consecrated organization of dedicated men and women who have been working behind the scenes."

19 *At mid-crusade and at its end, the people rallied in Yankee Stadium and Times Square, renewing themselves in their fathers' faith, and showing the world their trust in God.*

Thinking big is a characteristic of American enterprise. It drove railroads across our prairies and through the mountains, erected the Empire State Building, cleared the slums from Pittsburgh, and built a glittering Golden Triangle.

It gave us nuclear fission and blueprints of space ships.

It also filled the Yankee Stadium with a hundred thousand people in 93-degree heat on July 20, and a dozen city blocks about Broadway and Forty-second Street with 125,000 on September 1.

Thinking big is one of the things that come naturally to Graham and his associates.

On that hot afternoon of July 20, a religious reporter for the New York *Times* telephoned his paper's sports desk which ordinarily covered the ball park. "It's jammed full," he said. "People are standing hip to hip all over left field, right field, center field."

"Who is on first?" the sports writer cracked.

"Listen, this is the biggest crowd you ever saw. They're packed right up against the base paths."

"I don't believe it."

"Then don't say I didn't tell you!"

The sports writer said, "I don't believe it, but you might be right. I'll come out."

A congregation of one hundred thousand people!

Impossible!

"We know better. We handled 'em," a sergeant said, with the approval of eighty-three other uniformed officers and innumerable detectives.

"We seated them," said twenty-five hundred ushers.

"We saw them and sweated it out in the dugout," newsmen moaned.

They started arriving early. The first came about one o'clock. Some six hundred delegations from churches, believing that this was to be the last meeting of the crusade, had arranged for reservations for forty thousand seats. They came in four hundred busses, by car, subway, and on foot.

The *Times* reported, "They elbowed each other gently. When they stepped on each other's toes, they said, 'Excuse me.'"

By six o'clock, all of the sixty-seven thousand seats were occupied. Special guests were enjoying refreshments at an informal reception in the Stadium Club. And newsmen were fraternizing with members of the Graham organization in the Yankee locker room.

A stadium guard, checking up, wandered about seeking gate crashers. He encountered a young man without credentials. "Out you go," he said.

"But I'm on the team," the youth said.

"You're not kiddin' me," the guard snarled. "I happen to know the Yanks ain't in town."

"I'm on the Graham team. I'm a minister."

"Oh! Sorry, sir."

Just before seven o'clock, applause rose from the stands in a great crescendo as Billy Graham and Vice-President Richard Nixon approached the speaker's platform that had been erected over second base.

The invocation, led by the Reverend Dan Potter, of the Protestant Council of New York, concluded in a sound like summer thunder as a hundred thousand people repeated the Lord's prayer.

In the lower tier behind third base the four thousand massed voices of Cliff Barrows' combined choirs sang the "Hallelujah Chorus," then joined with Bev Shea in the most popular of all crusade songs, "How Great Thou Art."

When Vice-President Nixon spoke he said, "Billy Graham has asked me to say a few words. But I preside over a body where nobody says a few words." Then he added, "But I bring you a message from one who is a very good friend of Billy Graham and one who would have been here if his duties had allowed him, the greetings and good wishes of the President of the United States, Dwight Eisenhower."

A superb moment came when the evangelist sought the aid of all those present in carrying the crusade forward for three more weeks. "I would like for every Christian who will rededicate his life to God's cause to stand."

Almost half of the vast crowd stood in response, including every person on the platform behind Graham.

Graham's sermon was a passionate warning that "America is facing its gravest crisis in history." He said that America had been in danger of being destroyed as a nation four different times. The three earlier crises were the Revolutionary War, the Constitutional Convention in Philadelphia, and the Civil War. Causes of the present crisis were numerous but the gravest was "moral deterioration."

"Divorce, crime, juvenile delinquency, the breakdown of honesty and integrity, four million chronic alcoholics and a thousand and one psychological diseases plague the nation," he continued. "There is only one solution for our collective problems that can

175

guarantee the survival of America and its continued prosperity. Christ is the only answer . . ."

A few minutes before nine o'clock, it was time for the invitation. Observers saw the packed aisles, the blocked exits, the solid human mass that occupied the outfield from fence to fence, and wondered how anyone could come forward in that throng.

The evangelist asked for another form of declaration and the *Times* reported: "Because of the huge crowd, he [Graham] said that he could only ask those that 'accepted Christ' to stand or raise their hands if they were already on their feet.

"Slowly, over the Stadium, individuals rose, and couples got up. And in the outfield hundreds of hands slowly pointed upward. No accurate estimate could be made . . . there were hundreds and very likely thousands."

During the next three weeks over two thousand letters of decision came from the Yankee Stadium audience.

A record had been made and a climax reached. The people went slowly back to their busses, subways, and autos, as if reluctant to leave. And as they walked, a strange new sound was rising over clashing gears and shrilling police whistles. A hundred Gospel choruses were resounding through the song of the city.

No one will ever know the extent to which personal plans were changed by the decision to carry on. Some of the Graham team had to cancel trips to European religious rallies. Members of the executive committees hastily rearranged their vacation schedules. Ushers, counselors, and choristers by the hundreds abandoned out-of-town holidays and gave their services to crusade tasks.

Early in August, the Crusade Executive Committee made another fateful decision. George Burnham of *Christianity Today* magazine reported it in his syndicated column:

"The Billy Graham New York Crusade, a growing giant which the devil can't stop and God won't, has been extended through August. The Crusade's Executive Committee, in asking Graham to continue had a simple reason: how can we stop this tremendous thing that God is doing?"

"Billy Graham, badly in need of a rest after the most exhausting days of his ministry, was in full agreement with the committee that the Crusade must continue.

" 'Who are we to halt the opportunities made possible by God?'

176

he asked. 'There are many missionaries on foreign fields who have done far more work than I have done. They don't quit and come home when they get tired.'"

In mid-August he canceled all daytime appointments in order to preach directly to youth, spurred by the most outrageous teen-age delinquency the big city had ever seen. He recommended putting the Bible into every classroom. He called youth to march under Christ's banner, with results already disclosed in another chapter.

Amid the preparations for the final rally at Times Square he developed a specific proposal for handling teen-agers in trouble. Visiting Governor Harriman, he proposed that youth camps be set up on a semi-military basis with educational programs on Americanism and special courses of religious instruction.

Shortly, on August 29, it was time for a final press conference and a summing up.

The facts were impressive:

To date, 1,814,000 in attendance, the largest for any evangelistic effort on record.

Thus far, 53,626 decisions for Christ compared with 38,447 during the twelve-week period of the London campaign in 1954.

Of those who made decisions, 93 per cent were residents of the New York area.

And 22,000 were made by young people under twenty-one.

In other terms than statistics, Graham said he hopes his crusade has been "like a bomb opening the gates of the city to the infantry of the church."

"Many lives have been changed," he added. "It is noticeable by a smile on the subway instead of a frown. Thousands of people will carry Bibles all around town. Thousands of high-school students in New York will carry Bibles and Testaments to school in the fall. There have been more than 17,000 inquirers to finish our first Bible study course."

That night he pleaded with a capacity audience to carry on in the spirit of his campaign after his departure from the city on Sunday night. There must be "spiritual awakening and revival in every church in the city," he declared.

As August ran its course, a question often asked by crusade enthusiasts was, "What about the last meeting? How can you top Yankee Stadium?"

At first, no answer was forthcoming. But the query lighted a fire in some bright, inventive minds. Every open space in Manhattan was considered: Central Park had plenty of room but electrical facilities were lacking; Battery Park downtown was too difficult to reach; the United Nations hall . . . the campus at Columbia University. . . .

Someone said, "How about Broadway and Forty-second Street, the crossroads of the world!"

That was it! If America's play street could be turned into an outdoor temple for even one hour, what a symbol to the world that could become!

On the Sabbath evening of September 1, a multitude of tireless, dedicated groups undertook their final pilgrimage. From Staten Island, Brooklyn, Queens, the Bronx . . . from the Jersey shore and Jersey hills, from the salty flats of Long Island's south shore . . . executives from Westchester and Connecticut, fishermen, truck farmers, and dairymen . . . and the station-wagon set from suburbia.

The New York *Times* said:

"It was a smiling, well-mannered crowd that did not seem to mind being herded about a little by the police and ushers. They were quick to burst into song, quick to pray, and to break in little conversational groups.

"'I've been hearing about Billy Graham for years, and he has everything,' a woman about 40 said enthusiastically to a companion.

"'Well, you know the soprano part and so do I,' a teen-age girl remarked. 'But how are we going to get the pitch?'

"Seen from a roof forty-five stories above Broadway and 39th Street, the crowd looked like a stream of bright pebbles feeding slowly onto the black-surfaced avenue.

"At 6:40 P.M. they were packed almost solidly from 42nd Street to 38th Street. The tones of an organ carried skyward between the tall buildings. A setting sun glinted on the roofs, but the street was shadowy. 'Spectators, go to 38th Street,' a loudspeaker began insisting.

"Around the edges was a thin trickle of cynical Broadway dandies. Their favorite word was 'dead.' 'This is a dead show.' 'Look at those dead beats. So he saves you, so we'll be dead anyway in fifty years, if we don't get the bomb first.'"

And finally, with the assemblage packed into the narrow width of Broadway until they formed a living dagger thrusting into the heart of Manhattan, a half moon rose above the steel-and-concrete jungle, and Graham's last service commenced.

Here was the summer's final challenge to the evangelist. For the first time his wire and tape and gadgetry lay exposed to the naked eye. Electricians had argued noisily about where to place mikes. TV camera crews stepped on toes and swaggered into the best spots, with an obvious preference for union rules over the Ten Commandments.

Overhead, spider-web towers of iron carried huge lights to illuminate the TV picture, and the banks of loud-speakers to hurl sermon and songs through the Broadway canyon. Busses ground noisily along Forty-second Street, fifty feet behind the pulpit. As on the first night, so many weeks earlier, cameramen swarmed about the platform.

This was no outdoor cathedral, not yet anyhow. Around the busy platform, it was bedlam wired for sound. But down along the old cowpath now called Broadway the pilgrims stood in rapt anticipation. These were the faces one had seen in the Garden, the gentle eyes, the sweet smiles. Their hands clutched crusade bulletins as if holding something precious and fragile. When Cliff Barrows, now an old friend as well as their song leader, called for a show of song sheets, thousands of them fluttered overhead until, from above, it looked as if the thoroughfare were carpeted with sudden, swirling snow.

After announcements, Graham rose to his final challenge, his battle-ax swinging as fiercely as ever.

The *Tribune* said:

"Honky-tonk life, cheap souvenir stores offering nude statuettes, neon advertisements for liquor and holiday travel, all provided a frame for the evangelist. To the audience, he was literally a man who had literally turned his back on the Gay White Way which flashed and moved behind him."

The *Times* said:

"When the Rev. Dr. Billy Graham began to speak a few minutes later, the city had put on her spangled evening dress of white, red and blue lights. The preacher's earnest voice seemed to crackle along the canyon between the buildings."

"This is the spot that thousands of tourists think of as New York," Graham proclaimed. "Many foreign visitors judge America by Times Square. Scores of nationalities jostle each other, speaking many languages. Some stare in wonderment at the blaze of lights; others hurry along the streets to the theatres and places of amusements.

"Here in Times Square is the dope addict, the alcoholic, the harlot . . . along with the finest citizens of the world. It is primarily a place of amusement, money making, drinking, eating and making merry.

"Tonight for a few moments it is being turned into a great cathedral as a symbol of spiritual revival that is now in progress in America. Let us tell the whole world tonight that we Americans believe in God.

"Let us tell the world tonight that our trust is not in our stock pile of atomic and hydrogen bombs but in Almighty God.

"Let us tell the world tonight that we are morally and spiritually strong as well as militarily and economically. . . .

"Let us say also a prayer tonight for those millions that have no freedom.

"Let us tonight make this a time of rededication—not only to God but to the principles and freedoms that our forefathers gave us.

"On this Labor Day weekend, here at the Crossroads of America, let us tell the world that we are united and ready to march under the banner of Almighty God, taking as our slogan that which is stamped on our coins . . . 'in God we trust.'"

In this final service he dispensed both with a collection and the invitation to come forward. He asked only for those who wanted to make a decision for Christ to raise their hands. Thousands did so, and they were requested to mail in post cards so that the Graham team could put them in touch with churches.

While he was still preaching, the electric ribbon sign on the Times Tower, which flashes ticker-tape news day and night, spelled out the glowing words: "Billy Graham Crusade ends in Times Square Rally."

At nine, the crowd dispersed. By nine-thirty the street made quiet and beautiful by 125,000 pilgrims lay deserted and ugly.

The beauty was gone and the truth was gone . . . but both were flowing into homes and apartments all over Greater New York where men and women and young people were remembering things they had heard from beginning to end of the world's greatest crusade:

Graham's farewell at the Garden . . .

"In our spirit of dedication and in our spirit of humility and dependence upon the spirit of God, we may not see you again until we meet at Jesus' feet. What a time that is going to be! It won't be long for some of us. We'll all be there.

"What a hope we Christians have! Down here we have suffering, misunderstandings, many times persecution. But up there! Up there, the Bible teaches, the Church, in the coming of Christ, shall gloriously triumph. And if you are in Christ, you are on the winning side.

"Here, in this year of 1957, God has done a great work.

"To God be the Glory!"

And the still-echoing voice of George Beverly Shea as he sang at Times Square:

> "It took a miracle to put the stars in place.
> It took a miracle to hang the world in space!
> But when he saved my soul,
> Cleansed and made it whole,
> It took a miracle of love and grace."

20

Again the question: Were people changed? Would it last? Was New York touched? The final answer is years away. But here and now the reborn thousands answer, "Yes . . . yes! . . . YES!"

The long-range problem of Graham's evangelism has never been merely to win converts. As he saw, years ago, the main problem was to induct the new-born Christians into the Christian brotherhood, and to nourish them so they would grow to full stature.

In the early fifties, in co-operation with Dawson Trotman, president of the Navigators, a Bible study-by-mail group that originated among U.S. sailors in World War II, the first follow-up steps were planned and executed.

It was a giant stride forward, beginning with the decision card signed by every person who came forward, on which he indicated the church of his choice. This card became the trigger to a chain reaction of automatic but carefully planned follow-up steps.

1. A copy of the card went to the pastor of the church named, with a letter suggesting that the individual be visited within forty-eight hours.

2. A letter was sent a few days later to the pastor to ask if the individual had been visited. This was accompanied by a self-addressed and stamped postal, on which the pastor could report the results of his call.

3. A letter signed by Billy Graham was sent to the one who had made his decision, congratulating him on that decision and strengthening him in his resolution to follow Christ.

4. By phone, mail, or personal visit, the counselor who had assisted the inquirer to his decision made a follow-up contact to see if a satisfactory church relationship had been established.

In general, the plan worked only as well as the ministers of a community helped it to work. Graham had done all he could. Now his "babes" were in other hands. When calls were made promptly most converts joined a church. When they were given things to do that gave them significance and dignity in the Christian fellowship they matured and remained faithful.

But many pastors were slow to make calls and many churches were neglectful of the newborn once the name was on the roll. The drawback, Graham perceived, was a lack of corporate enthusiasm for evangelism, plus the usual affliction of people being busy, lazy, or smug.

The New York Crusade introduced what may prove to be a most effective device for upsetting this indifference. It is called visitation evangelism and it adds the warmth of personal interest to the dynamics of Graham's preaching at the Garden.

"We may never have this momentum again," the evangelist said in July, while considering the pros and cons of continuing the crusade into the hot month of August.

Visitation evangelism takes advantage of that momentum, to carry a church ahead in an atmosphere wherein teen-agers are carrying Bibles and women in supermarkets are talking about Christ.

In New York this last phase of the crusade became the responsibility of a special committee under the chairmanship of Dr. Jesse M. Bader.

Again, the eleven areas of Greater New York were divided into fifty useful subdivisions, each with a director.

Again, by mail and personal appeal, churches were urged to co-operate in a program of house-to-house visitation.

Dr. Bader described the new philosophy when he said, "We have been ringing church bells when we should be ringing doorbells. We have been doing by proxy what we should be doing by proximity. And some have tried to do by purse what they should be doing in person."

Visitation evangelism is evangelism at the grass roots.

Each co-operating church organized its own list of "prospects" from those who had never joined the church but who came to Sunday school, had a child in the school or a baby on the Cradle Roll, were occasional attendants, were non-church members in the family of a member, attended various church affairs, or contributed to the budget.

Workers were chosen and instructed—fourteen for each hundred names on the "Responsibility List"—and for the four days and nights from October 20 to 25, they met, received their assignments, and went forth two by two to ring doorbells with a mission that was surely as praiseworthy as those other marchers who do the same for Polio, Red Cross, and Community Fund drives.

As this is written, the results are still coming in. Churches by the hundreds are co-operating. Graham returned to New York to preach during the week of September 23 at suburban rallies held in armories, parking lots and football fields. His final service would be a gigantic rally at the Polo Grounds on Reformation Sunday, October 27.

Among the persons to be visited will be those of the fifty-six thousand Garden converts who, according to meticulously kept records at headquarters, have not joined any church.

Could this massive visitation program provide the long-sought link between mass and personal evangelism? Graham prays that it will. Whatever the result, this final step expresses his philosophy that the claim of Christ on man must first be presented simply and with authority, and afterward the church, by its own testimony, nurtures the newborn in Christian living.

Will the church do this?

Will the people really find spiritual security in their decisions and rededications?

Over one million letters came to Graham during the Crusade. Here is one of many that give a clue.

This Long Island commuter wrote:

"I must confess, when the subject of the Billy Graham Crusade first came to my attention, I did not know what to do. After prayer I felt that the Lord would have me go to the counseling classes. It was not long before all of my questions and doubts were erased from my mind.

"At the Garden . . . another counselor and I made a habit of going out for a sandwich before each meeting. For a reason unknown to us, we both decided this night to go to a different place. By the leading of the Lord, we ended up in a drugstore on Broadway.

"There we saw two Italian sailors who couldn't speak English. Somehow, we got them to the Garden. In looking around for someone who could speak Italian, I found a layman from the Church of the Nazarene in Valley Stream. I took him to our two sailors and then asked other counselors to pray for them and for the interpreter who would not only have to counsel but translate the message.

"After the invitation, having the two young men on my heart, I found it difficult to counsel. And I sat around with the hope of seeing one of them in the counseling room. Praise God for his goodness and answer to prayer. On that night, both young men accepted Jesus Christ. To see the change in their faces is indescribable.

"To complete the story, we counselors became good friends with them and they have a permanent invitation to our homes any time they are in New York.

"The second incident concerns one Sunday afternoon when our family was going to the crusade. We got on the subway, but our trip was interrupted by mother nature's call to one of our young children. While I waited for them to rejoin me, I heard a young Negro airman asking directions from someone nearby. Recognizing immediately that the information he received was incorrect, I redirected him and we struck up a conversation which got around to the crusade.

"When I invited him to come with us, he said he could not make it. He was on his way to his base and was trying to catch a bus, the last that would get him there in time.

"Right then and there I prayed about this. Then I heard what must have been the Spirit of God say, 'The Lord will provide.' When I repeated these words, he accepted my invitation to the Garden.

"During the service, I watched him as I prayed for him. When the invitation came, I kept waiting for him to go forward. My wife, also watching, said, 'Why don't you go talk with him?' I replied, 'No, I've done my share in bringing him here.' I continued to watch and wait and still he didn't go.

"Finally, I decided that if I were going to counsel that night I would have to go on to the counseling room. As I passed his seat, the same voice that had said, 'The Lord will provide' now said, 'If you don't ask him, he won't go. His soul is in your hands.'

"With these words, I could not argue. So I spoke to the young man, about his soul and getting right with God. It took practically nothing more than the invitation, and he went forward immediately.

"What a blessed time! We were both richly blessed that night. Later, after leaving him with an adviser, a group of us went out for a bite and I stopped at a newsstand which was next to a bus terminal. Very seldom did I buy a paper after the meetings, but this night I had a desire for one. And there stood my airman. He had a smile on his face that would have lit up Madison Square Garden.

"I asked him about his transportation problem. He said, 'You told me the Lord would provide. Well, I've just found a bus leaving here in fifteen minutes that will get me to the base one hour earlier than that other one.'

"God's hand must have been on that lad, for if I had left home earlier, if my wife had not gotten off the train with the children, this wonderful experience would never have taken place.

"Though we can never see further ahead than right now, the Lord can.

"It would not be fair for me to close this letter without giving credit to the one who helped so much. To go to the crusade, I had to get up at 5:30 A.M., go to work and leave directly from work for the Garden. Seldom did I get home, after taking others home, before 12:30 or 1:00 A.M. When I left in the morning, my wife was asleep. When I got home, she was asleep. This made it very lonely for her and the children. Her sacrifices and prayers were one of my biggest assets.

"Statistically speaking, these figures are as near to being right as I can humanly make them.

"Number of meetings attended 85
"Number of people counseled 87
"Number of miles traveled by car and subway 9600
"Cost of transportation ....$273.
"Donations, approximately ....$80.

"Giving God all the glory and asking his Blessing on that which you are now undertaking, I am, in the name of Christ, Yours truly . . ."

Some of the letters were short but equally personal, like this one from the pastor of a New Jersey church:

"I would like to share with you one of the greatest joys of my life. Last night, our daughter, a college graduate, now enrolled at N.Y.U., for her Master's, informed us that she had accepted your offer to stand up for Christ at a meeting two weeks ago.

"For a number of years she had struggled with the problem of life investment. She had gone off by herself many times to the woods and to the hills. But she never talked about it with me or her mother or anyone that I know of. She appeared to be drifting farther and farther away from us, and we thought farther away from Christ also.

"Last night she told us the whole story. In the Garden she gave her life to full-time Christian service, and upon completion of her studies at N.Y.U. she will apply for missionary service.

"We are very happy and I know this will bring a bit of joy to you also.

"Thank you, Billy. God bless you!"

And what of the larger concerns, the benefits to church, community, and society.

William Randolph Hearst, Jr., editor in chief of the Hearst newspapers, wrote:

"As an observer, reader and newspaperman, it was heartening to have an event with such a potential of hope, when so many others these days carry such a potential of despair.

"The final headlines called attention, and quite correctly, to the fact that it was the biggest evangelical crusade in the history of New York, and cited the hundreds of thousands of persons who attended the gatherings and the thousands who made the decision for Christ. I consider Dr. Graham's crusade a success from beginning to end.

"I think the final test is that Dr. Graham left New York a better city than he found it."

Mrs. Norman Vincent Peale, long-time resident and church worker with her celebrated husband, said:

"I have lived in New York City for twenty-five years, and through my church and interdenominational contacts have had opportunity to appraise the spiritual life of the city for a quarter of a century.

"I would like to testify that never in this period of time has there been anything even remotely approximating the profound spiritual impact which Billy Graham has made on New York City.

"For the first time there has been a definite soul searching on the part of people who heretofore have been, perhaps, not indifferent, but lacking in a deeper sense of the demands of the Lord upon their lives.

"I have never seen prayer take hold as it did in the days preceding the crusade, and as it continued all the way through. It is a great vindication of our faith that where you get a sufficient number of Christians to pray for a definite spiritual objective, amazing results are obtained."

Governor Price Daniel of Texas said:

"I thank God for the work Billy Graham is doing for the Lord's cause, and also what he is doing in behalf of this country around the world. I believe he is making people of the world understand what Americans really believe in."

The Rockefeller Foundation's executive vice-president, Lindsley F. Kimball, said:

"Billy Graham comes to New York. Through his own great humanity, understanding, and utterly fearless directness of purpose, through his obvious personal fellowship with God himself, and through world-wide prayer, miracles are wrought in the lives of many thousands—salvation is here and now for all who will. Billy, even as Saint Paul of old, insists, 'For I determined not to know anything among you, save Jesus Christ, and Him crucified.'

"New York itself is born again for two million souls who have found the Way, the Truth, and the Light."

Dr. Daniel A. Poling, who had defended Graham's ministry against early critics, summarized his conclusions in these words:

"Never before has New York City experienced anything approaching the Billy Graham New York Crusade in the authority of its impact upon this vast community. No area of our life has been immune to the crusade's influence and every segment of the city has been moved.

"Now it remains for the co-operating churches—more than seventeen hundred of them—to carry out the follow-up program that, with care and Christian statesmanship, has been planned for more than two years ahead. I know of one congregation in Manhattan that, during the first half of the crusade, received more than five hundred cards. To bring these thousands of new converts into the Church, to nurture and train them for their Christian testimony and service is at once the supreme obligation and opportunity of our faith.

"Here is a man who with his entire team is filled with the passion and purpose of his evangelical faith—an open channel for the Holy Spirit."

No individuals had greater knowledge of the scope and depth of Graham's work than those who labored closely with him on the committees appointed by the Protestant Council.

George Champion, president of the Chase Manhattan Bank and chairman of the General Crusade Committee, said:

"This will be a better world only when people accept the teachings of Christ and live accordingly. No legislation will fundamentally change individuals—the change must come from within their hearts and there is no set of rules or regulations to guide us like the Sermon on the Mount or the Ten Commandments. From the thousands who have come forward at the meetings I am sure the churches will receive the new vigor and strength which are so vitally needed in New York."

Charles H. Tuttle, distinguished lawyer and member of the Executive Committee, stated:

"No human analysis can exhaust or measure the full meaning of the stupendous religious phenomenon which the city of New York has just witnessed. Here has been indisputable proof before the eyes of all that two thousand years have not lessened the victorious and redemptive power of the Gospel Story, faithfully told with all its own directness, simplicity, and authority. So told, the people, as we have just witnessed, always hear it gladly."

A director of the Executive Committee, Dr. Frank E. Gaebelein, said:

"Since May 15, we have seen criticisms leveled at the crusade answered one after the other, until the only valid explanation of what has been happening at Madison Square Garden is that the Spirit of God has been using His dedicated servant, the devoted members of the team, the sacrificial efforts of thousands of counselors, choir members, and multitudes of prayer-helpers throughout the world, to face New York, and through New York the nation, with the claims of the Lord Jesus Christ in a new and living way.

"Results? Who can measure the impact of the tens of thousands who have been personally reached for the Lord. And while they are, despite their great numbers, only a minority in our secular culture, nevertheless the God who has brought them to Himself can be trusted to work in them through His Spirit to revitalize homes, strengthen churches, and bring to communities new dimensions of Christian living.

"To say that the New York Crusade is a success is inaccurate and inadequate. It has been a miracle. As the psalmist said, 'This is the Lord's doing; it is marvelous in our eyes.'"

From the Reverend John S. Wimbish, of New York's Calvary Baptist Church, came this evaluation:

"It is impossible to fully evaluate the impact of the Billy Graham New York Crusade on our community, for even the multiplied thousands of decisions reflect only the immediate results.

"If the increased attendance, quickening of interest, and receptiveness to the message of the Gospel which is being experienced at our church are any criteria, certainly the New York

Crusade has moved this city closer to God and has made at least a segment of its teeming population aware of things spiritual."

The Reverend Richard Allen Hildebrand, of the African Methodist Episcopal Church, declared:

"The Billy Graham New York Crusade was perhaps the most magnificent thing that ever happened to this great city.

"It was a clear demonstration of the power of prayer. We saw what God can do with mere humanity when we allow Him to use us. The sincerity and complete dedication of the evangelist are perhaps the chief reasons for his effectiveness.

"The crusade seems to have awakened a hungering and thirsting after righteousness throughout the City. Religion is easy discussion in almost every circle of society. Church attendance has increased remarkably.

"The crusade in ten weeks seems to have done more toward developing a sense of oneness among Protestants than years of planning and study have accomplished.

"May God ever bless Billy and his wonderful team."

Captain Conrad E. Jensen, of the New York City Police Department wrote this moving testimony:

"From the very first 'Counselor's Class' I attended I was thrilled with the evident blessing of God on the crusade. As the instructors taught the Word verse by verse, they covered territory I had been over before—yet I drank it in like a sponge and looked for more.

"Then came the night of May 15. At the conclusion of the message as Billy gave the invitation I peeked between my fingers and saw folks coming forward to accept Christ as their own personal Savior. It seemed unreal and unnatural. As I walked down the ramp with my adviser's ribbon on my chest, the smell of the circus greeted me. Then came the seeming confusion of the counseling room. I wondered, 'Can God work in all of this noise and seeming confusion?' I soon found out. What a joy it has been to work there night after night. Many of the experiences I shall never, never forget. One night I spoke to a twelve-year-old Puerto Rican boy who told me he came forward because he wanted Jesus in his heart—then turned to talk to a man, fifty years of age, who was a Sunday-school Superintendent and Church Treasurer and yet knew he had never been saved, and then told me tearfully that finally he had come to Christ.

190

"I've prayed with drug addicts and housewives—thieves and businessmen—young and old, and only God can take a cross section like this and make them all children of His.

"I'm supposed to be a 'tough cop' yet I fought back the tears (sometimes unsuccessfully) a number of times during the crusade when the Spirit of God has thrilled my soul beyond description.

"My opinion of the crusade might have little value to anyone else—but I know in my own heart that God was in it from start to finish. All I can say is thank God for this little 'foretaste of Glory.'"

Dr. Jesse M. Bader, general secretary of the World Convention of Churches of Christ (Disciples), declared:

"I consider the Billy Graham New York Crusade an unforgettable, history-making event in the life of New York, where I have lived for over twenty-five years. We have had no religious event among our Protestant Church of Greater New York since the days of Billy Sunday.

"This evangelistic crusade has been a blessing to New York. The city needed something of this dimension and nature in order to get the attention of a community of twelve million people of which only about one million are Protestant. Many Protestant ministers have been encouraged and many churches have been strengthened spiritually and numerically.

"I have never seen the Protestant ministers and churches more united on anything during the past quarter of a century than on this crusade. They have worked, prayed, and planned together. All through the Garden meetings, there has been the utmost reverence. There were no claptrap methods used in the services.

"It should be remembered that if there had not been an active, well-staffed Protestant Council of Churches, composed of over 1700 congregations, there would not have been a Billy Graham New York Crusade. It was through and with the Council that the crusade was held."

The Reverend David J. Fant, general secretary of the New York Bible Society, said:

"For the past thirty-seven years it has been my privilege to minister in New York City as pastor of three churches, religious editor and publisher, and now General Secretary of the New York Bible Society. From my watchtower I have viewed the Billy Graham Crusade as the biggest thing for the Protestant Christian cause that has struck our city during that long period of time. In the midst of materialism, worldliness, crime, and spiritual indifference it has descended upon us like a fresh breeze from heaven. Its benefits have been many: the winning of thousands to Christ; the witness of evangelical Christianity in a city that is largely Catholic, Jewish, and unchurched; and importantly, the uniting of the Protestant churches of our city in the primary mission of the Church—the winning of men and women to Christ."

John W. Bradbury, D.D., editor of the National Baptist Journal the *Watchman Examiner,* stated:

"As one among many who prayed over the years for the evangelization of New York City I am filled with thankfulness to God for the Billy Graham Crusade. It is the answer we sought. New York has been moved Godward. The effect of this campaign will be far-reaching. Many churches have now evangelical fervor they did not manifest effectively before. The cause of evangelism, as the emphasis upon salvation for the people, is alive in this city to a degree unequaled in more than a generation. Scores of thousands of people needing Christ Jesus as Savior have responded.

"I feel that God has granted New York a token of His mercy, using Billy Graham and his loyal team to lead this great metropolis to, at least, consider its duty to God."

Paul Moser, executive secretary of the National Council of Presbyterian Men in the U.S.A., said:

"Churchmen, including theologians, should be grateful for the emphasis of the speaker and the crusade throughout its entire organization on the necessity, for those who wish to continue in Christian maturity, to join a church. It is not important what anyone thinks about Billy Graham. It is important what you can hear on the streets of New York as men hum and whistle 'This is my story—this is my song—praising my Savior' or, in the apartment next door to you. What think ye of Billy Graham? When you study the faces of people as they go from Madison Square Garden to their homes and in their homes in many cases go to their knees with one prayer 'Make me a captive, Lord, and then I shall be free; Force me to render up my sword and I shall conqueror be,' there can be but one answer to that question, it is amazing what God hath wrought!"

Dr. Henry Perry, Executive Secretary of the American Tract Society and an active crusade adviser, said:

"Apart from the thrill of seeing thousands of inquirers pass through the counseling room where it was my pleasure to have a very small part, the joy of praying with new converts from all walks of life shall remain with me always.

"Equally as thrilling, however, was to observe the spiritual growth in passive Christians who now have fully accepted the challenge of our Savior before He ascended into glory, Acts 1:8 'Ye shall be witness unto me.'

"It will be fully a decade before the full impact shall be known."

Gayle J. Lathrop, executive vice-president of the Y.M.C.A., said:

"I had the privilege of hearing Mr. Graham on several occasions. He gave himself unstintingly during the sixteen weeks of the New York City Crusade. God used him to touch helpfully the lives of thousands of our citizens. I am sure that the laymen and pastors of many struggling Protestant churches and agencies like the Y.M.C.A. in the metropolitan area will find a more favorable climate in which to work. More lay people will be available to help if we have the vision, courage and faith to relate them to significant and relevant tasks."

Dr. John A. Mackay, president of Princeton Theological Seminary, at Princeton, New Jersey, made this encompassing declaration:

"It matters nothing whether the crowds were primarily made up of people with no church affiliation whatever, or that they were composed of nominal church members, or of devoted Christian men and women eager to show their interest in a cause. Something unusual has happened. No amount of propaganda by high-powered advertising methods, no super organization, no degree of natural curiosity, no mass psychosis, is sufficient to account for the throngs that went to listen to a young man deliver a simple, straightforward religious message. This thing has been of God.

"I have been equally impressed by the Christ-centered message of the evangelist. Jesus Christ has been set forth as the Savior from sin and the Lord of life. Men and women have been brought face to face with the Person in whom God revealed His love and power to mankind, and to whom, as the crucified and Risen Christ, they should commit their lives; for it is Christ alone who can change life.

"The 'new man in Christ,' who is brought into a very personal relationship to God, is the basic answer to the human problem. This 'new man' Billy Graham seeks, through the power of God, to bring into being. What becomes of the 'new man,' will depend upon a process of Christian nurture and education, for which the Churches must assume primary responsibility. If this obligation is accepted and worthily discharged, the converts in the Graham campaign, and those whose lives have been revitalized, will be fitted to accept their personal responsibility in the affairs of the Church and of society at large.

"As for the evangelist himself, I have the profoundest faith in God's servant, Billy Graham, not only as regards the quality of his personal Christian character, but also as regards his view of the essential mission which God has committed to him. For that reason I give my unqualified support to the work in which he is engaged."

The Reverend Dan Potter, executive director of the Protestant Council which initiated the crusade, in the closing days, pinpointed these tangible results in relation to its four major objectives.

1. To win men to Christ:
. . . With more than fifty-five thousand who have come forward to date . . . there is no question in my mind that this crusade is winning men to Christ. This response is many times more than I dreamed possible.

2. To make our city God-conscious:
. . . There has never been a time in the history of the Protestant Council when the metropolitan area was more God-conscious. It is almost as easy to talk about Billy Graham and the Spirit of God as it is to talk about the weather.

3. To strengthen the churches:
. . . Forty-four per cent from among those who committed themselves to Christ at Madison Square Garden were not church members. Virtually all of these inquirers are taking instructions and being taken into membership in various churches.

4. To make New York City conscious of moral, spiritual, and social responsibilities:

. . . Dr. Graham has spoken forcefully on the race issue, housing, alcoholism, narcotics, corruption, gambling, crime, communism, atomic-bomb experimentation, disarmament, and many other issues. While the detailed solution of these issues has not been championed, it has been made clear over and over again that personal salvation is only the first step . . . In light of the progress made, I feel humble and grateful to Almighty God.

Thus spake some of the leaders of the world in which we live. Each is informed, accurate, and authoritative. Each spokesman represents a segment of importance and responsibility.

And yet there are the others, the untouched and unchurched, who still cannot comprehend the reality of the New Birth. To them the crusade remains a mystery, a good show, but still a mystery.

God gives understanding, Graham has said, only after man accepts Jesus Christ by faith.

Then, with the inflowing Holy Spirit, understanding comes and with it the power that turns a man about until, like a stone tossed into a pond, its cleansing ripples of right living wash through families and communities and nations until at last the whole world is clean.

STEPS TO PEACE WITH GOD

1. RECOGNIZE GOD'S PLAN—PEACE AND LIFE

   The message in this book stresses that God loves you and wants you to experience His peace and life.

   The BIBLE says . . . For God loved the world so much that He gave His only Son, so that everyone who believes in Him may not die but have eternal life. John 3:16

2. REALIZE OUR PROBLEM—SEPARATION

   People choose to disobey God and go their own way. This results in separation from God.

   The BIBLE says . . . Everyone has sinned and is far away from God's saving presence. Romans 3:23

3. RESPOND TO GOD'S REMEDY—CROSS OF CHRIST

   God sent His Son to bridge the gap. Christ did this by paying the penalty of our sins when He died on the cross and rose from the grave.

   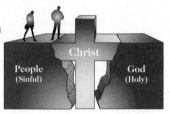

   The BIBLE says . . . But God has shown us how much He loves us—it was while we were still sinners that Christ died for us! Romans 5:8

4. RECEIVE GOD'S SON—LORD AND SAVIOR

   You cross the bridge into God's family when you ask Christ to come into your life.

   The BIBLE says . . . Some, however, did receive Him and believed in Him; so He gave them the right to become God's children. John 1:12

THE INVITATION IS TO:

REPENT (turn from your sins) and by faith RECEIVE Jesus Christ into your heart and life and follow Him in obedience as your Lord and Savior.

PRAYER OF COMMITMENT

"Lord Jesus, I know I am a sinner. I believe You died for my sins. Right now, I turn from my sins and open the door of my heart and life. I receive You as my personal Lord and Savior. Thank You for saving me now. Amen."

If you are committing your life to Christ, please let us know!
Billy Graham Evangelistic Association
1 Billy Graham Parkway, Charlotte, NC 28201-0001
1-877-247-2426 • www.billygraham.org